W9-ACS-380

# Society in
# Colonial North Carolina

Charles II, after ten years in exile, returned to England in 1660 and was crowned in 1661. His quarter-century reign was marked by commercial and territorial expansion. Charles granted a large tract of land, including much of present-day North Carolina, to eight Lords Proprietors in 1663. Portrait photograph from the files of the Division of Archives and History.

# Society in Colonial North Carolina

Alan D. Watson

Raleigh
Division of Archives and History
North Carolina Department of Cultural Resources
Revised Edition, 1996

© Copyright, 1996, by the North Carolina Division of Archives and History

ISBN 0-86526-267-5

# Contents

# Maps and Illustrations

# *Foreword*

The Historical Publications Section is pleased to issue a new, revised edition of Alan D. Watson's *Society in Colonial North Carolina.* The section published the first edition in 1975 and reprinted it in 1982. The booklet sold out again in 1989 and, despite its popularity, has remained out of print.

*Society in Colonial North Carolina* describes day-to-day life in North Carolina before the American Revolution. It discusses such topics as education, health, recreation, religion, transportation, town life, marriage, and death. For this revised edition, the author provides a new chapter entitled "Servitude and Slavery." New illustrations further enhance the text.

Dr. Watson, professor of history at the University of North Carolina at Wilmington, is a familiar figure to students of North Carolina history. He has published a number of titles with the Historical Publications Section, including four county histories. He also has written numerous articles for the *North Carolina Historical Review* and other journals, as well as major books on New Bern and Wilmington. He earned his doctorate at the University of South Carolina.

In the production of this edition of *Society in Colonial North Carolina,* Dr. Watson has been ably assisted by Lang Baradell and Lisa D. Bailey of the Historical Publications staff. Mr. Baradell edited the revised manuscript, compiled an index, and saw the volume through press. Ms. Bailey applied her considerable proofreading skills to the project.

Joe A. Mobley
*Administrator*
Historical Publications

January 1996

CHAPTER ONE

# SETTLEMENT, CLASS, AND CHARACTER

After two unsuccessful efforts in the 1580s to settle North Carolina, the colony received its first permanent white inhabitants in the 1650s. These early colonists were Virginians who pushed their colony's boundary southward as they settled in the Albemarle region to establish a fur trade with the Indians of the area and to take advantage of fertile land for farming. In 1663 Charles II of England granted land, including the Albemarle and future North Carolina, to eight prominent Englishmen. Some of these men had assisted the king in his exile and aided his accession to the throne. The Lords Proprietors, as the new owners were called, were the beneficiaries of a royal determination to enlarge English holdings overseas, which would expand English trade, promote the Protestant Church, and add luster to the reputation of Charles II.

The Albemarle remained the center of settlement throughout the early proprietary era. Efforts by a group of Barbadians and New Englanders to establish a colony along the lower Cape Fear between 1664 and 1667 proved abortive. By the 1680s, however, resident North Carolinians and immigrants appeared below the Albemarle Sound, gradually moving southward to the Pamlico and Neuse Rivers. The establishment of Bath Town in 1705, the Baron Christoph von Graffenried settlement at New Bern in 1710, and the incorporation of the town of Beaufort in 1723 reflected that activity. The Cape Fear enterprise of Gov. George Burrington and Maurice Moore in the

Anthony Ashley Cooper (left), Earl of Shaftsbury, and Sir William Berkeley, who served as governor of Virginia for almost thirty-five years, were two of the eight Lords Proprietors. The charter granting these men control over the territory known as Carolina is shown below the portraits. All photographs from the files of the Division of Archives and History.

Maurice Moore, a military and political leader in colonial North Carolina, was instrumental in establishing a permanent settlement in the Lower Cape Fear. Portrait photograph is from Samuel A'Court Ashe's *History of North Carolina*, vol. 1 (Greensboro: Charles L. Van Noppen, 1908), 570.

1720s finally inaugurated permanent settlement of the southeastern part of the province.

Population in North Carolina increased slowly as settlements spread along the Atlantic coast. The number of inhabitants rose from ten thousand in 1700 to twenty-one thousand in 1720. The whites were a diverse people. English predominated, but Welsh, French, Swiss, German Palatines, and Scotch-Irish constituted minority groups. The Welsh in the late 1720s and early 1730s colonized an area on the Northeast Cape Fear River known as the Welsh Tract. The French were Huguenots (Protestants) from Virginia who arrived as early as 1690 or 1691 to settle near the head of the Pamlico River. Another group of Huguenots settled along the Trent River in the first decade of the eighteenth century. The Swiss and early Germans arrived principally with the de Graffenried expedition. Scotch-Irish appeared in small numbers as early as the 1670s.

North Carolina lured immigrants from England, mainland Europe, the West Indies, and other continental colonies. The newcomers sought cheaper and more fertile land, a more temperate climate, religious toleration, and freedom from political oppression. While some improved their circumstances, even prospered, many found life harsh. The vagaries of the weather, conflict with Native Americans—

particularly the devastating Tuscarora War, 1711-1714—and illness, among other factors, played havoc with their hopes and dreams.

When the Crown purchased North Carolina in 1729, the colony contained approximately 36,000 inhabitants after seven decades of existence. Thereafter population rose markedly. The provincials numbered between 65,000 and 75,000 in 1750 and between 175,000 and 200,000 in 1770, though some estimates place the number at a quarter of a million or more at the time of the Revolution. Although the high birthrate of Carolinians contributed to the rapid rise in population, immigration also helped bring about the fivefold or more increase in settlers during the royal era.

Observations concerning the extraordinary influx of settlers came from sources within North Carolina and from outside the colony. Gov. Gabriel Johnston in 1751 reported numerous people immigrating to the colony, and three years later Gov. Arthur Dobbs told English authorities that hundreds of wagons had entered North Carolina from the northern colonies. Virginia minister James Maury wrote that during 1755 over five thousand Virginians had crossed the James River headed for North Carolina and that three hundred had passed the Bedford County courthouse in one week during 1756.

The pace of immigration continued unabated in the 1760s. Benjamin Franklin in 1763 wrote that some ten thousand families had moved from Pennsylvania to North Carolina in the preceding decade. In 1766 Gov. William Tryon erred little when he stated that North Carolina was being peopled more rapidly than any other colony. In fact, only Georgia, which had started from a much smaller base population, exceeded North Carolina's population growth rate. Although some immigrants settled the remaining vacant land in the eastern counties, the majority planted in the western regions of the colony. This led a Virginia newspaper to report that "There is scarce any history, either antient [sic] or modern, which affords an account of such a rapid and sudden increase" of population.

The new colonists represented diverse nationalities, languages, social classes, and economic groups. While the preponderance of the immigrants were English, the Scots, Scotch-Irish, and Germans constituted significant minority stocks. The Scots who came to North Carolina after 1730 were "the earliest, largest, and most numerous settlement of Highlanders in America." More interested in joining relatives or friends than in seeking western land, the Scots were the only large, non-English nationality to come directly from their native land. The migration from Scotland to North America began after the Act of Union in 1707, continued throughout the remainder of the colonial era, and peaked in the early 1770s. Economic distress was the major stimulus prompting the Scots to come to America, though political retribution in the wake of the Scottish defeat in the Battle of Culloden in 1746 may have contributed to the exodus.

The number of Highlander immigrants before 1763 is impossible to determine. Between the end of the French and Indian War and the beginning of the Revolution approximately twenty-five thousand Scots left their homeland. More than five thousand came to North Carolina. Fifty-four shiploads of Scots arrived in the colony in the summer of 1770 alone. By 1775 the estimated number of Scots in the province ranged from ten thousand to twenty thousand.

The Scottish immigrants included Highlanders and Lowlanders. The latter were far less numerous but disproportionately important because they included many merchants who played a significant role in the colonial economy. The Lowlanders scattered throughout the province, but the clan-conscious Highlanders concentrated in a well-defined area in the upper Cape Fear Valley, which comprised the present counties of Anson, Bladen, Cumberland, Harnett, Hoke, Moore, Richmond, Robeson, Sampson, and Scotland. Subsequently, the Highlanders extended their settlements westward to the land between the Catawba and Yadkin Rivers.

The Scotch-Irish, that is Scots or descendants of Scots who had settled in Ireland, emigrated for various reasons. The Woolens Act of 1699 dealt a severe blow to that industry in Ireland, the Test Act of 1704 militated against the unlimited practice of Presbyterianism, and excessive rents for farms and widespread famines caused distress in the rural areas. A Pennsylvania newspaper in 1729 referred to the inhabitants of Ulster when it stated that "Poverty, wretchedness, misery, and want are become almost universal among them."

Although most colonies received some Scotch-Irish, Pennsylvania was the most popular due to its fertile land and tolerant religious policies. From the Pennsylvania entrepôt the Scotch-Irish fanned out through the Appalachian foothills and valleys. They utilized the "Great Wagon Road," which began at the Schuylkill opposite Philadelphia, ran westward through Lancaster to the Susquehanna River, then wended through the Shenandoah Valley in Virginia to Staunton Gap, crossed the Dan River in North Carolina, and terminated at the Yadkin River. At that point other roads spread through western North Carolina and into South Carolina. Some Scotch-Irish entered North Carolina from the south. They disembarked at Charleston and followed the trading routes to the backcountry to reach the northern province.

The Germans followed the Scotch-Irish route to the Piedmont of North Carolina. Although they represented various religious denominations, the Germans generally regarded themselves as a distinct group in the province and were more zealous in confining their settlements to western North Carolina than any other group of immigrants. Religious, political, and economic distress forced thousands of Germans to flee their native land in the early 1700s. Some who came to North Carolina sought cheaper land; others intended to establish self-contained communal villages. The Moravians exemplified the latter. Their tract of land of almost one hundred thousand acres, known as Wachovia, was settled in 1753. The North Carolina colony was an extension of the Pennsylvania Moravian group, in which the brethren practiced communal ownership of property and mutual cooperation.

The African American presence soon accompanied that of the European in North Carolina. Slavery had begun to develop in Virginia by the time that colony's residents pushed into the Albemarle, and the Lords Proprietors subsequently encouraged slavery in the Fundamental Constitutions. The settlement of the Cape Fear in the 1720s was led to a great extent by immigrants from South Carolina, a colony where slaves constituted half of the total population. Thus slavery rather naturally emerged in North Carolina, where it became entrenched in a colony whose economy rested on such labor-intensive crops as tobacco and rice and such industries as naval stores.

The number of African Americans remained relatively small during the proprietary era but increased rapidly after the mid-eighteenth century. From about one thousand in 1705 and six thousand in 1730, their numbers accelerated to the point that blacks constituted perhaps a quarter of the population by the Revolution. Though natural increase was responsible in part for the growth of the African American population, importation of slaves from the neighboring

*Newbern, December 20, 1774.*
*Just imported in the* SCHOONER HOPE,
Thomas Foster, *Master, from* AF-
RICA, *a Parcel of likely healthy*

# SLAVES,

CONSISTING of Men, Women, and
Children, which are to be sold for Cash, or
Country Produce, by EDWARD BATCHELOR
& Co. at their Store at UNION POINT.

This advertisement for the sale or barter of slaves recently brought from Africa appeared in the *North Carolina Gazette* (New Bern), February 24, 1775.

colonies of Virginia and South Carolina and from the West Indies and Africa may have accounted for half or more of the increase. African origins are often obscure, but slaves were sometimes identified as Guinea, Angolan, Ibo, Mandingo, or Coramantee, indicating that they represented virtually the entire slaving coast of western Africa. Continuing importations meant that during the quarter century before the Revolution about half of the adult slave population had been born in Africa. That in turn ensured the continuation of African cultural characteristics among blacks in North Carolina.

Slaveholding, as indicated by the number of black taxables, was most prominent in the Lower Cape Fear River valley area. A large percentage of families in that region owned slaves, and their average slaveholdings were larger than those in other areas of the colony. The percentage of slave-owning families in the Albemarle was only slightly lower than that for the Cape Fear, but the number of slaves per household was distinctly smaller. Slaveholding appears to have been relatively widespread in the north-central portion of the colony; few slaves, however, were found in the west.

Slaves not only constituted an increasing proportion of the total population but became concentrated in larger numbers on farms and plantations. By 1771 over 60 percent of bondsmen lived on plantations with ten or more slaves, which meant that they could maintain an African culture and create a semblance of community and family life apart from masters and mistresses. Nonetheless, blacks and whites necessarily shared the colony of North Carolina, and the result was an interplay of language, religion, food, and many other features of life that brought forth a society neither European nor African, but American.

The seemingly endless influx of immigrants and their servants and slaves re-created the stratified societies of Europe. Although the English mainland colonies in general, and North Carolina in particular, seemed quite democratic by eighteenth-century standards, society was nevertheless structured into a hierarchy of classes: the elite or gentry, the "middling" class, and the lower or "meaner" sort of people. Bertie County exemplified the disparities of wealth. There the poorest 30 percent of the population owned 1.7 percent of the wealth and the richest 10 percent, 58.8 percent.

Socioeconomic differences, education, family lineage, political connections, and worldly sophistication distinguished the classes. The gentry, composed of the leading planters, merchants, and professional men, was the smallest of the three groups. The gentry lived well, at least by North Carolina standards, and provided political as well as social and cultural leadership for the colony. The middle and lower classes constituted the most numerous segments of the populace. The former consisted primarily of smaller farmers and merchants, less prestigious professionals, and town artisans. The lower order included the very poor farmers, tenant farmers, day laborers, and similar dependent members of society. The life-styles of the middle and lower orders betrayed their inferior wealth and breeding. They were kind, hospitable, and generous; yet they were also rude, noisy, and uncouth.

Below the three primary classes and outside the prevailing social structure lay the indentured servants and slaves. Indentured servants fell into two classes: voluntary and involuntary. The former were poor people who bound themselves to a labor contract for three to five years in order to pay their passage to America. The involuntary servants were paupers, convicts, and political prisoners who were shipped by the English authorities to the colonies where they were sold under similar contracts of longer duration. While serving their masters the servants enjoyed a status little better than that of chattel. However, they did possess some rights, including the assurance of adequate food, clothing, and shelter. At the end of the period of indenture, masters were required to give the servants "freedom dues," which consisted variously of barrels of corn, suits of clothes, guns, or money.

Slaves represented the nadir of the provincial social system. As a form of property, slaves were subject completely to the will of their masters. Not until 1774 was there legislation to prevent the purposive slaying of a slave, and the penalty for the first offense was only twelve months imprisonment. Every apparent aspect of a slave's life—food, clothing, shelter, marriage, travel, work, leisure—from birth or importation depended upon the owner's inclinations. One of the most pitiful scenes in the province was the slave auction block, where humans were examined like animals, and families, including young children, were separated forever.

Despite the authoritarian structure within which they lived, slaves often managed to create their own society. Marriages were arranged and approved by masters, but slaves established private family relationships. Under adverse circumstances male slaves often dominated and disciplined their families. Religious activities quickly became important to them. Slaves also enjoyed their own forms of recreation, including dancing, singing, and games. Masters came to respect the limitations of slave endurance, inasmuch as the price of ignoring customary Sunday and Christmas holidays, for example, was likely to be work slowdowns, broken agricultural implements, and abused animals.

For many slaves the burden of bondage became unbearable. Advertisements for the recovery of runaway slaves filled the newspapers. Descriptions given by the owners indicated white attitudes toward those slaves bold enough to challenge the slave system. Runaways were termed surly, cunning, artful, and flippant. The advertisements also showed that many slaves had overtly protested their enslavement. The back of one runaway evidenced the frequent discipline of the whip; another had recently suffered a broken arm due to a blow to the elbow. Many runaways made good their escape, while others committed suicide rather than return to bondage.

Free blacks occupied an uncertain position in society among free whites, bond servants, and slaves. Blacks became free in a variety of ways. Some were runaway slaves, mostly from other provinces, who passed for free persons in North Carolina. William Byrd and his surveying party found a family of blacks who "call'd themselves free, tho' by the Shyness of the Master of the House, who took care to keep least in Sight, their Freedom seem'd a little Doubtful." Some slaves were freed by will, deed, or legislative prescription. Faithful or meritorious service prompted most acts of manumission, although free blacks often purchased wives, children, and other relatives in order to free them. The children of miscegenation (racially mixed unions) greatly added to the number of free blacks. Such offspring took the status of their mothers, and in many instances white women bore the children of black, often slave, men.

Free blacks were subject to various forms of legal discrimination, including an excessive tax burden. Wives, black and white, as well as the daughters of free black males were subject to taxation, unlike the wives and daughters of whites. The inordinate tax burden provoked protests from many residents, including whites, of Granville, Edgecombe, and Northampton Counties, but effective reform did not materialize. Free blacks could not testify in court against whites and probably were excluded from jury duty. Yet they bore the same responsibilities for defending and supporting the government, which included militia duty and working on public roads.

Continual immigration in conjunction with various economic handicaps experienced by North Carolina prevented the upper class domination found in Virginia and South Carolina and contributed to a society characterized more by its middle and lower classes. Shortages of capital and skilled labor and the failure to develop a staple crop impeded economic growth and the concentration of wealth. These factors were compounded by a dangerous coast that restricted trade and communication. While North Carolinians raised tobacco and rice and became England's principal supplier of naval stores, they were never able to develop an economy grounded firmly on a staple such as tobacco in Virginia and rice and indigo in South Carolina.

The greatest impediment to trade and immigration was a coast guarded by barrier islands called the Banks or Outer Banks. Only relatively shallow inlets admitted shipping to the sounds and thence to the mainland. One major river, the Cape Fear in the extreme southeastern region of the colony, emptied directly into the Atlantic, but its entrance was guarded by dangerous shoals. Only half of North Carolina's export trade left by its own ports; the remainder passed

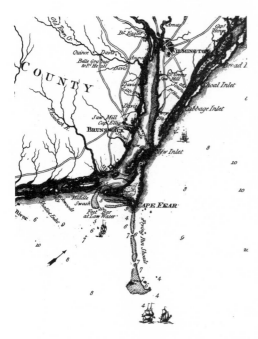

The Cape Fear River provided an outlet to the Atlantic Ocean, but its usefulness as a trade route was compromised by the presence of hazardous shoals near the mouth. This drawing of the mouth of the Cape Fear River is from "An Accurate Map of North and South Carolina ... by Henry Mouzon and Others," published in London in 1775 and in Paris in 1777.

through Virginia and South Carolina markets. Reliance upon neighboring colonies meant higher freight costs, reduced profits for exports, and greater markups on imported goods. The value of per capita exports from North Carolina on the eve of the Revolution was less than half that of Virginia and only a fifth that of South Carolina.

Of course, North Carolina's economy improved greatly during the course of a century of colonial development, but it remained disappointing to many. Shipping advanced, the number of slaves increased, and markets expanded. Yet at the end of the colonial era writers almost uniformly commented negatively when describing economic prospects: "want of ports ... must ever keep [North Carolina] comparatively low"; "very little Advances made even yet"; "far behind the neighbouring Provinces in Industry and application." Rather than offering quick riches, North Carolina's economy more likely betokened disappointment or at best provided opportunity for minimal improvement.

Other factors adversely affected economic progress in the colony. An unhealthy environment, at least along a coast marked by swamps and poorly drained marshlands; high, regressive taxes; a lack of ready money; and the usual affliction of droughts, floods, and other natural phenomena haunted the colonials. Despite the rapid peopling of the colony, too little labor was available to make proper use of the vast amounts of land being claimed. As Declaration of Independence signer William Hooper remarked, "North Carolina is a striking Exception to the general Rule . . . that the Riches of a Country are in Proportion to the Number of Inhabitants."

North Carolinians turned to slavery and to a lesser extent indentured servitude to augment the labor supply. One Cape Fear resident wrote in 1743 that the lack of slaves to cultivate the land encouraged poverty. Although slaves increased in number and in percentage of the total population during the eighteenth century, they paled into insignificance compared to the slave populations of Virginia and South Carolina. Only in the Lower Cape Fear, Neuse–Trent area, and parts of the Albemarle did slaves reside in considerable numbers. Not surprisingly, in those areas, particularly in the Cape Fear, a more leisured, sophisticated, and cultured white society emerged.

Still, North Carolina displayed a population composed predominantly of small to middling farmers. The majority of whites, 70 to 80 percent, owned land, but few claimed estates of a thousand acres or more. When they did, most of that land was uncultivated because of the paucity of labor or because it was marginal or wasteland. Without slaves, remarked one observer, "Lands are of little Value." A French traveler wrote in 1765 that the bulk of the estates he viewed in North Carolina were of "no advantage or value for the present."

Limited slave ownership likewise reflected a comparative lack of wealth in the colony. Only a minority of families owned slaves. Slaveholdings tended to be small except in the Lower Cape Fear counties of New Hanover and Brunswick, though even there few (William Dry, 128; George Moore, 118; Richard Quince, 113) possessed more than a hundred taxable slaves. Tax lists for eleven counties in North Carolina show that during the 1770s and 1780s less than 1.5 percent of families owned twenty or more slaves. By comparison, 6 percent of Virginia families and a higher percentage in South Carolina owned twenty or more. Bonded labor was the clear avenue to riches, but a road available to few in North Carolina.

Other than planting, the occupations of merchant and lawyer offered opportunities for advancement. But North Carolina merchants

North Carolina's assembly first authorized the issuance of paper money during the administration of Gov. Edward Hyde, 1711-1712. Notice the warning, "Death to Counterfeit," in the margins of this later twenty-shilling note. From the files of the Division of Archives and History.

appeared to lack necessary business skills in the estimation of their peers beyond the province. Many in North Carolina were small operators who lacked the capital "to keep the branches of their Commerce in vigour," according to Charleston, South Carolina, merchant Henry Laurens. Some prospered, however, for Samuel Cornell of New Bern acquired a "very considerable fortune" twenty years after he arrived from his native New York in 1754.

While the legal profession included such Chowan County luminaries as Samuel Johnston, Jasper Charlton, and James Iredell, most North Carolina lawyers encountered criticism in and beyond the province. James Murray in 1736 wrote that "This country . . . exceeds all ever I heard of [in] the West Indies for bad Attorneys." Richard Henry Lee of Virginia claimed that lawyers were "bad everywhere" but worst in Carolina. The North Carolina General Assembly in the

1770s referred to growing "Mismanagement of Causes" by lawyers, either through ignorance or neglect. Although the number of attorneys was small, perhaps forty-five in the mid-1760s, and litigation was rife, few seem to have been able to take advantage of their opportunities to amass considerable estates.

By the end of the colonial era socioeconomic differences were more obvious, but society remained less stratified than in Virginia and South Carolina. The French traveler in 1765 remarked that there were "very few if any rich people" in North Carolina, "a fine Country for poor people, but not for the rich." Gov. William Tryon in 1768 described the best estates as "very moderate." The Latin American patriot Francisco de Miranda, in visiting New Bern in 1783, concluded that the "social system," even in that large, reasonably cultured town and port, was "still in its swaddling clothes." Although society in the Lower Cape Fear boasted the greatest concentrations of wealth and evidenced greater aristocratic demeanor, Janet Schaw on the eve of the Revolution found a "most disgusting equality" during her visit to the region.

Recreational pursuits distinguished the various elements of society yet often brought them together in "democratic" fashion. In the west, men gathered for logrollings, house-raisings, and corn shuckings, while women engaged in quilting bees and spinning matches. Sports such as jumping, wrestling, footraces, and quoits, a game similar to horseshoes, occupied males at public gatherings. The lower orders engaged in their notorious wrestling matches, in which North Carolinians prided themselves on their ability to scratch, bite, kick, and gouge out eyes. By the mid-eighteenth century Gov. Gabriel Johnston called the legislature's attention to the advent of the "barbarous" sport of boxing in the colony.

All classes enjoyed dancing, particularly when fiddles or bagpipes could be obtained for accompaniment. Although the genteel appreciated the ever popular reels and hops, they also staged more formal dances. Lawyer Waightstill Avery participated in a "splendid Ball" one evening in 1769 in the town of Halifax. When James Milner was selected to represent Tarboro in the provincial assembly in 1772, he gave an elegant supper for the leading gentlemen of the town and Edgecombe County, followed by a ball, "which was greatly embellished by a very numerous and brilliant Appearance of most charming Ladies."

Cockfighting and horse racing were popular diversions that united all classes. When possible, Carolinians obtained their cocks from England or Ireland. Where this was impractical or impossible, they raised their own blooded stock. The fights were well advertised. On the day of battle people came from as far as twenty miles away to participate in the festive, though barbarous, event, where the genteel and the lowly rubbed shoulders as they shouted, cursed, drank, and bet their money.

The popularity of cockfighting was rivaled only by that of horse racing. Colonials in the South exhibited great concern over their racing stock, and North Carolinians were no exception. Quarter racing, an exercise in sheer speed with two horses racing a quarter mile, was the most prevalent form of racing in the colony. Of course, North Carolina racing did not enjoy the reputation of that in Virginia or South Carolina, but the wealthy in the colony imported European breeds and crossbred their own stock to best advantage. Abner Nash of New Bern advertised his horse Telemachus for stud service on easy terms in order "to encourage the Gentlemen Farmers of this Part of the Province the more readily to enter spiritedly on this very profitable and public spirited Business of breeding good Horses, as their Neighbors of Halifax, Virginia, and other Places, have done before them."

The importance attached to horse racing is difficult to overemphasize. Robert Howe of Wilmington, later a renowned Revolutionary patriot general, was said to have starved his family in an attempt to save enough money to make an impressive showing at the Virginia races each year. When Willie Jones of Halifax courted Sukey Cornell, he found that Sukey's father, Samuel, a wealthy New Bern merchant, would not allow his daughter to marry a man who would risk a fortune on a horse race. Jones thereafter declined any further courtship since racing was his favorite amusement and he would under no circumstances forgo that pleasure. Racing, then, in North Carolina was frequent, competition keen, and the stakes often high. While gentlemen bet large sums on the outcome, the less affluent, white and black, wagered a shilling or two, a quart of rum, or even a drink of grog.

Gambling, whether on horse races, card games, billiards, bowls, shuffleboard, or board games such as backgammon, was exceedingly popular in early North Carolina and often transpired in taverns where

Willie Jones of Halifax, a
wealthy planter and future
political leader, ended his
courtship of Sukey Cornell
rather than submit to her
father's demand that he give
up betting on horse races.
Portrait photograph from
the files of the Division of
Archives and History.

men of all ranks of society came together. Not only did taverns offer respite to travelers and refreshments to those nearby, they also served as places to conduct auctions and slave sales, as repositories for the public mail, and as centers for political deliberations. Although taverns served many positive functions, they often evoked images of drinking, brawling, and wagering.

During the colonial era gambling in North Carolina became so widespread that the provincial assembly passed legislation to curb its excesses because it discouraged work, corrupted youth, and strained family ties. Billiard tables beckoned to many, including James Iredell of Edenton, who recorded in his diary that he usually lost money at the game. Francisco de Miranda noted the penchant of Carolinians for billiards, remarking that every town through which he passed had two or three public tables. Miranda found that Carolina wives often berated their husbands for spending too much time at that "French custom."

Perhaps the attraction of gambling, the reliance on slavery, the debilitating climate, and the sickly populace along the coast helped to explain the reputation of North Carolinians for indolence. As the aristocratic Virginian William Byrd helped to survey the boundary between his colony and North Carolina in 1728-1729, he left the following description of Carolinians in his diary:

The Men, for their Part, just like the Indians, impose all the Work upon the poor women. They make their Wives rise out of their Beds early in the Morning, at the same they lye and Snore, till the Sun has run one third of his course, and disperst all the unwholesome Damps. Then, after Stretching and Yawning for half an Hour, they light their Pipes, and under the Protection of a cloud of Smoak, venture out into the open Air; tho', if it happens to be never so little cold, they quickly return Shivering into the Chimney corner. When the weather is mild they stand leaning with both their arms upon the corn-field fence, and gravely consider whether they had best go and take a Small Heat at the Hough: but generally find reasons to put it off till another time.

Thus they loiter away their Lives, like Solomon's Sluggard, with their Arms across, and at the Winding up of the Year Scarcely have Bread to Eat.

To speak the Truth, tis a thorough Aversion to Labor that makes People file off to N Carolina, where Plenty and a Warm Sun confirm them in their Disposition to Laziness for their whole Lives.

While Byrd obviously exaggerated, others echoed his sentiments. Janet Schaw, a Scotswoman who visited in the Cape Fear on the eve of the Revolution, declared that if the men "can raise as much corn and pork, as to subsist them in the most slovenly manner, they ask no more." Laziness may have characterized those living in the east, but inhabitants in the western area evoked a more favorable reaction. People in the backcountry were described as "good farmers and very worthy people," "hardy and laborious Races of Men," and bold and resourceful with impressive athletic ability. In almost every instance, however, as indicated by Byrd, the women were deemed the more industrious of the sexes.

Although North Carolina and its people suffered from a host of critics throughout the eighteenth century, the "levelling" spirit, middle class society, and economic opportunity found favor among many within the province. The absence of an entrenched elite and the wide distribution of property eroded the deference to superiors that might have been expected in a highly stratified society. Byrd wrote that North Carolinians "are rarely guilty of flattering or making any court to their governors but treat them with all the excesses of freedom and familiarity." Indeed a sort of tenuous equilibrium existed between upper and lower classes in which violent disorder might ensue if the masses felt their freedom threatened by the elite. The rapid peopling of a frontier inevitably brought the individualism, acquisitiveness, contentiousness, and provincialism that so marked the Carolinians, though those same features also characterized most colonial Americans.

CHAPTER TWO

# FAMILY

The family was the principal unit of social and economic life in the colonies. It brought order and stability to emerging settlements, transmitted and maintained cultural traditions, and served as the focus for the mainly agrarian, small-enterprise, preindustrial economy. Over the years the family structure, norms of behavior, and psychological expectations of family members changed. All the while the rigors of the colonial enterprise and a frontier existence tested the endurance of the family.

Historians of the family in early America define the family or household as an independent economic entity, the members of which lived in one dwelling, or in close proximity, and submitted to the authority of the "head" of the unit. Thus the family might consist of nuclear members, extended members, nonrelations, wards, apprentices, servants, and slaves. This definition of the family has been assumed for purposes of perspective and comparison.

Population data from the eastern counties of Craven, Chowan, Bertie, Onslow, and Carteret, mainly from the 1740s, and a partial census from Pitt County in 1775 help to detail the size and composition of the family in early North Carolina. The average size of the family in the five counties was 7.3, while that for Pitt County was 7.6, suggesting little variation in size during the middle years of the eighteenth century. Most families contained from three to nine persons. Over 90 percent comprised fewer than fifteen individuals, and families of twenty or more were rare.

While whites predominated in North Carolina, slaves constituted an increasingly significant component of the colonial household. The number of whites per household in the five eastern counties ranged from 4.5 to 6.3, averaging 5.5. Pitt County figures closely approximated those of the eastern counties. Slaves were found in 37 percent of the families in the eastern counties and 42 percent of the families in Pitt County. They accounted for approximately one-fourth of the total population.

Elsewhere in North Carolina slaves exerted a greater impact on family size. In those counties in which 40 percent or more of the households contained slaves—Bertie, 1768, 1774; Brunswick, 1769, 1772; Chowan, 1772; New Hanover, 1755, 1763, 1767; Perquimans, 1772—family size was significantly larger than in poorer eastern counties and the newly settled western areas. Excluding the Lower Cape Fear (New Hanover and Brunswick Counties), the percentage of families containing slaves appears to have increased as the Revolution approached, indicating that slaves had become an increasingly important part of the colonial household.

The Lower Cape Fear region proved an anomaly in that the number of slaveholding families remained stable. A larger percentage of the families in the region owned slaves, however, and the number of slaves owned by individual families was much greater than in other areas of North Carolina. In New Hanover and Brunswick Counties as many as 12 to 20 percent of households contained forty slaves, and bondsmen constituted more than 60 percent of the total populace. Demographically and in other respects, the Lower Cape Fear more closely resembled the South Carolina Low Country, from which it was originally settled, than the remainder of North Carolina.

Servants, though far less numerous than slaves, also increased the size of households. A vague term that applied to sundry persons, servants included indentured immigrants, apprenticed orphans, those bound to labor according to private contract, and occasionally day laborers. In Bertie County in 1763 and 1768, taxable servants (white males age sixteen and over and black males and females age twelve and over) were present in at least 20 and 29 percent of the families, respectively. Few families contained more than one servant, none more than four.

Free blacks and mulattoes constituted a small but distinct part of the populace. Their numbers varied widely among the counties, but they were most prominent in the developing western region of the province. Even there, however, free blacks rarely constituted more than 3 percent of the total taxable population. In the western counties the size of free nonwhite families appears to have been larger than the average in North Carolina; in the principal slaveholding eastern counties, such as Chowan and New Hanover, family size was smaller than the average.

The formation of African American slave households proved difficult. One of the earliest slave families in North Carolina was that of Manuell and his wife Frank, listed in the 1695 inventory of former governor Seth Sothel. They became the property of wealthy planter Thomas Pollock in the Albemarle, who later owned several slave families, including Scipio, his wife Moll, and their two sons. Manuell and Frank, who had five children, lived somewhat independently. They hired themselves out and owned property, including a bed and gun. But Manuell and Frank were unusual, for male slaves outnumbered females during the colony's early years and not until about 1755 was the ratio sufficiently balanced to permit large numbers of slaves to form families, and that occurred mainly in the eastern counties.

Naming patterns among slaves reveal their determination to maintain family life in an uncertain existence. Many of the male and female slaves owned by Jean Innes in 1761 were named for their parents, as evidenced by the names George Junior, Sinclear Junior, Delia Junior, and Dinah Junior. Fifty-one of the seventy-eight slaves owned by New Bern merchant John Wright Stanly at his death in 1789 belonged to family units.

Fragile though it was, the slave family became an institution of great consequence for bondsmen, providing emotional satisfaction and the opportunity for the perpetuation of African culture. Although such unions lacked legal support and were subject to dissolution at the discretion of master and mistress, the owners had a vested interest in maintaining the family unit, for marriage and family may have made slaves more satisfied with their lot in life and less likely to run away. Nonetheless, all too often slave families—husbands and wives, parents and children—were split when dictated by economic need, death of owners, or marriage of master or mistress.

On the whole, households in North Carolina were smaller on average than those in the British island colonies but slightly larger than those in New England and the Middle Atlantic provinces. White males headed the vast majority of the families, which centered on the nuclear unit, though extended kinship ties remained very strong. Marriage was the ultimate expectation of most in the colony. James Iredell wrote that "in this Country a young Man without the joys of a private Family leads a very dull, and I may add, a less improving Life." Women perhaps sought similar emotional and social satisfaction from marriage. Moreover, given the limited economic opportunities available to them, females must have found marriage difficult to avoid.

Respect for the institution of marriage varied greatly in the province. Among the more genteel, highly formal courtships preceded the marital union. Iredell wooed Hannah Johnston for more than a year before asking her brother, who was also her guardian, for permission to marry, and then the wedding did not take place until another year had elapsed. Where organized religion made little impact on the populace, formal matrimonial ties were lightly regarded. After visiting the North Carolina backcountry Anglican minister Charles Woodmason wrote, "Polygamy is very Common—Bastardy, no Disrepute—Concubinage General."

Although lovers increasingly made their own choice of marriage partners in the eighteenth century, parents occasionally controlled prospective unions. Justina Davis, fifteen, shed many tears at the thought of ignoring her true love to marry seventy-three-year-old Gov. Arthur Dobbs, but her parents would not allow her to miss the opportunity to wed a royal governor with a considerable estate. Nancy Rainbough of Edenton opposed her match with innkeeper John Horniblow, but her parents forced the marriage.

Still, youthful passion was not always easily channeled. Penelope Johnston eloped to marry John Dawson after her guardian objected to the marriage. James Murray's opposition to the marriage of his niece to William Hooper was ignored. And the mother of a Miss Moseley, a young girl from a reputable family in the Lower Cape Fear, pleaded in vain that her daughter renounce her intention to marry the illegitimate son of a Captain Monroe.

Although many married young, and John Brickell believed that the woman who remained unmarried at twenty was "reckoned a stale Maid," North Carolinians often postponed nuptials until they reached their twenties. A study of Perquimans County marriages from the settlement of the county to 1740 showed that the median ages at marriage for men and women were twenty-three and twenty, respectively. The North Carolina figures were comparable but somewhat lower than those for New England and other mainland colonies. One determinant of marriage age was the death of the father. Surviving children tended to marry later because of the additional household responsibilities imposed by the demise of the head of the family.

Within marriage men apparently dominated the household. In colonial society Judeo-Christian tradition was reinforced by the institutionalization of English common law, which considered husband and wife as one. Single women—femes sole—were legally independent, free to execute deeds, sue in court, act as guardians, and make wills. The legal identity of married women—femes covert—was subsumed by their husbands, except in unusual instances in which married women acted as surrogate husbands—femes sole traders.

Some wives tried to avoid their impending subservient status in marriage by concluding prenuptial contracts to protect their property rights. A systematic study of such pre-Revolutionary agreements found in New Hanover County deed books reveals that they were few in number and confined principally, though by no means exclusively, to the upper class. Moreover, over 70 percent of the contracts involved widows, an indication of the desire of those women to preserve a measure of the independence gained through widowhood and to secure their property for the benefit of the children of the previous or future marriage.

The most striking characteristic of the marriage agreements was their diversity. Each was devised for a particular circumstance. Jean Innes reserved property for her use during her lifetime and the power to direct the disposal of half that estate by will. The property to be received by Isabella McAlister from her previous marriage was to be placed in trust for her two children by that marriage. Mary DeRosset, with the approval of her future husband, Adam Boyd, transferred certain property to trustees "For the securing and settling [of] a competent maintenance for the said Adam Boyd and Mary DeRosset. . . ."

Nevertheless, in seventeenth- and early-eighteenth-century North Carolina married women may not have been too severely disadvantaged. In the colony's developing frontier society widowhood and remarriage were frequent, the legal system was in its infancy, and public life was less institutionalized. As a result, domestic and public roles were less distinct and more subject to overlap. Many activities, including business and religious affairs, took place in the home where women might be involved. Many married women appeared in various capacities in the courts of the colony. Some, including Ann Marwood Durant of Perquimans County, acted as early as the 1670s as attorneys-in-fact representing their husbands in legal matters.

Religion, ethnic background, geographic location, and social status helped to determine gender expectations within the family. Quakers encouraged women to be outspoken and independent, treating them as equals in the home as well as in the meetinghouse. The Presbyterian Scotch-Irish and Scots, reflecting the Calvinism of their church, viewed husbands as dominant. Along the frontier, both in the Albemarle during the early days of settlement and in the backcountry in the eighteenth century, gender roles remained fluid.

Along the coast and in the more settled regions of the colony in the eighteenth century the status of wives diminished as family and gender roles became more carefully delineated. As North Carolina evolved from a primitive frontier outpost to a more stable colony within the British Empire, women in and beyond marriage found fewer opportunities to participate in the legal system. This was the result of a less flexible application of English common law and the appearance of professional attorneys. The increasing separation of private and public spheres of life left women, married and single, fewer opportunities to assert themselves. And changes within the household—larger houses, more privacy, more children due to lower mortality rates, more servants and slaves—meant increasing domestic responsibilities for wives.

In contrast to their counterparts in the backcountry, men and women in the longer settled areas occupied distinctive domains. This was particularly true among the elite. Francisco de Miranda, writing from New Bern in 1783, observed that married women maintained "a monastic seclusion and a submission to their husbands such as I have never seen." Their "entire lives are domestic," he stated, and they separate themselves "from all intimate friendships" to devote themselves "completely to the care of home and family." Janet Schaw praised her sister-in-law, who lived on a plantation near Wilmington, as a model of "domestic accomplishments," meaning that she was "a most excellent wife and fond mother."

Of course, exceptions attested to the rule. Mary Harnett, wife of the well-to-do merchant and Revolutionary patriot Cornelius Harnett, not only tended the traditional household garden but sold minced pies, cheesecakes, and biscuits in Wilmington and supplied the townspeople with eggs, poultry, and butter. Housewives were among the seventy professional spinners identified in Rowan County between 1753 and 1790. And the Edenton Tea Party in 1774 showed that women had developed a political consciousness sufficient to compel them to declare openly their support for the incipient revolution.

Still, concern for home and care for children occupied the attention of most married women. They gave birth approximately every twenty-four to thirty months, though, of course, infant and child mortality took its toll. In the Pitt County census of 1775, white children constituted 41 percent of the total population and 54 percent of the white population. The average of 3.2 children per household in Pitt County at least equaled the mean number of children per family in the mainland colonies and easily surpassed the norm for the island provinces. Only 9 percent of the Pitt families had no children, a low percentage compared to the other British colonies.

Among the children, orphans often claimed the attention of local authorities. Legislation placed responsibility for such young ones with their respective county courts. The courts apprenticed orphans whose estates were nonexistent or too small to support them and found guardians for children with greater means. Between 1757 and 1775 the Edgecombe County court directed the care of 283 orphans, of whom 95 or one-third warranted apprenticeship.

When the courts apprenticed orphans, they bound them to masters or mistresses until the boys reached the age of twenty-one and the girls eighteen. The apprenticed orphans were to learn a trade or "Suitable Employment." Masters and mistresses agreed to provide the orphans with proper food, clothing, lodging, and the rudiments of education. Apprenticeship of impoverished orphans served an indispensable function in relieving the county and parish of the burden of supporting the children, while preparing the orphans to enter society as useful adults with the fundamentals of an education and a skill.

The county courts attempted to cushion the shock of the loss of a father and dissolution of the family by finding relatives or friends to care for apprenticed children. The courts further eased the transition by apprenticing siblings to the same master when possible. That was particularly true for illegitimate offspring, indicating a sympathetic understanding on the part of the authorities for the more difficult adjustments to be made by those children. The courts often bound boys or girls of like age and circumstance to the same master in order that the orphans might enjoy the companionship of peers.

Some children who lost their fathers possessed sufficient inheritances to pay for their care and tutelage. The courts made every effort to leave these children, particularly the young ones, in the care of their mothers. Where it was impossible to rely upon maternal supervision, the courts attempted to place them in homes of relatives and friends. Custom dictated, however, that once an orphan reached fourteen years of age, he or she should be allowed to choose a guardian. Nevertheless, orphans attaining that age rarely elected to leave their court-appointed guardians.

The study of orphanage in Edgecombe reveals a widespread incidence of illegitimacy, lending credence to the hypothesis of some historians that the mid- to late-eighteenth century was a time of relatively free sexual behavior in America. Of the 95 apprenticed orphans in Edgecombe County between 1757 and 1775, at least 35, and perhaps 39, were illegitimate. Several women and men habitually engaged in sexual relations outside the bonds of marriage. During the twenty years before the Revolution as many as ten women had two or more illegitimate children, including Elizabeth Boazman who bore five illegitimate offspring by 1768.

Beyond Edgecombe some of the most prominent men in the province, including Cornelius Harnett, fathered children out of wedlock. After Harnett's death the mother of his illegitimate daughter asked his executors to appoint guardians "to do justice and be friendly to my unfortunate daughter as much for her father's sake as for her own sake." Whites occasionally took black mistresses, and according to a visitor to the Cape Fear region in 1773, "no reluctance, delicacy, or shame [was] made about the matter." In New Bern, John Carruthers Stanly, a prosperous mulatto, was generally assumed to be the son of wealthy merchant John Wright Stanly.

Child-rearing practices differed among families and were influenced by social class and ethnicity, among other factors. Still, in the eighteenth century greater life expectancies for children and parents as well as increasing wealth tended to produce homes in which children were the center of attention and parents were often indulgent. Penelope Dawson once wrote that her "bratts have been all in full cry," but she was a devoted mother to her young ones whose father had recently died. A German minister in the backcountry observed disapprovingly that the English allowed their children to grow up like domestic animals. Janet Schaw, upon bringing the children of John Rutherfurd to Wilmington, found that the father, a plantation owner and royal officeholder, was "as much in love with his daughter as I expected, . . . and so fond of the boys, that I fear they will be quite spoiled."

Children manifested their freedom in various ways. When Christian Newton stole several articles of clothing from a store in Edenton in 1728, her attorney offered "youthful folly" as a defense of her actions. Less harmful, though offensive to the public, was an incident in the same town in 1737 involving two young couples who were called before the Chowan County court for swimming nude in the Chowan River. Four decades later James Iredell, patriot and jurist, wrote Nelly Blair of Edenton, a young lady for whom he served as a father figure in the absence of her deceased parent, that her mother hoped she "would take a good deal of pains to bring . . . her volatility, at least some of the time, down to a reasonable standard."

Family turmoil came from a variety of sources. Husbands and wives occasionally sought sexual satisfaction beyond the bounds of marriage. Parish and county court records are replete with instances of cohabitation, adultery, and bastardy. In 1719 the grand jury of the general court of the province presented John Myers and James Boulton for "Seduceing" the wives of Thomas Portis and William Jennings Sr., respectively, and for living with them. An agent of a British mercantile firm, while touring the backcountry in 1753, learned that the wife of a Granville County justice of the peace had given birth to seven children during her marriage, two of whom her husband had refused to acknowledge as his own.

Certainly married life was not always idyllic, threatened as it might have been by infidelity and loneliness. Younger, charming, and often away from home on circuit, lawyer James Iredell apparently embarrassed his wife Hannah in what might have been "a silly flirtation." Though the nature of the matter is unknown, Iredell apologized and a stronger marriage resulted from the incident. While riding circuit, Iredell and his brother-in-law Samuel Johnston once visited Richard Bennehan and his new bride in Orange County. They found that Mrs. Bennehan had "not a single women she can associate with nearer than Hillsborough," which was eighteen miles away, and tears came to her eyes when Johnston indicated that he might bring his wife to visit.

Often wives feared for their personal safety at the hands of their husbands. Mary Wall of Bertie County went to court in 1762 to complain that her husband had beaten her and threatened her life. She had good reason to be fearful, for John Jones of the same county had been executed four years earlier for murdering his wife. When faced with complaints such as those by Wall, the courts placed the offending husband on recognizance accompanied by a bond with securities to ensure his proper conduct for the term of a year.

When the dangers, disappointments, or rigors of marriage became intolerable, husband and wife might have resorted to separation or divorce. The latter, however, was almost impossible. In North Carolina the legislature did not enact a general divorce law until the nineteenth century, and divorce petitions were rarely presented to the provincial legislature before the Revolution. Solomon Ewell was virtually alone in his request to the assembly in 1766 for a dissolution of his marriage because his wife had eloped and lived adulterously.

Ewell's wife, however, was one of many who seized the initiative in marital squabbles. Early in the eighteenth century the Reverend John Urmstone declared that many women left their husbands to come to North Carolina and live with other men. Later Vinkler Jones stated that his wife had left him "with an intent to ruin him"; Morris Connor declared that his wife had departed his household and had "otherwise treated me ill." Conversely, the courts entertained many petitions from wives whose husbands had forsaken their families, leaving the women and children with no means of support.

For some the parting was more amicable. When Ephraim and Ann Vernon in New Hanover County "mutually agreed to separate and live apart from each other," the husband deeded two plantations, six slaves, and sundry household goods to his estranged wife in order that she "should live reputably and comfortably." Joseph and Mary McGehe of Bute County advertised their separation of 1769 in a New Bern newspaper, the *North-Carolina Gazette*, and Henry and Catherine McLorinan of Wilmington recorded their separation of 1775 before the New Hanover County court.

In the case of separated couples, husbands were expected to provide for their wives. Some complied, but in 1731 the Bertie County court had to direct Fincher Hayne to appear to answer a complaint brought by Anne Hayne for nonsupport. In 1749 Onslow justices ordered the goods belonging to Joseph Paul to be delivered to his estranged wife "for her Use and Comfort." The following year Jennet Boyd told the provincial council that her husband deprived her of "any subsistence [intending] to reduce . . . [her] to the utmost Misery in her old Age."

Whether from divorce, desertion, or widowhood, single women headed some colonial households. Their number was small, never amounting to more than 10 percent of the total in any county and usually ranging from 2 to 5 percent. These figures were low compared to those in other British colonies. The more recently settled western counties of Anson, Cumberland, Granville, and Orange had the fewest female heads of households. Families headed by women were usually smaller in size than the average, though such women were more likely to own slaves.

The central problem faced by widows was the need for economic support. In North Carolina, where an agrarian order mandated extensive manual labor, as many as one-fourth to one-third of the widowed families contained free whites, age sixteen years or older, other than the widow. Most were the sons of the widows, though some may have been servants or apprentices. Slaves were more prominent. Seventy percent of the households headed by women contained bondsmen. Not only did that figure exceed the norm for North Carolina households, but the average number of slaves in families headed by women easily surpassed the average for households generally.

In addition to labor, widows needed housing and other benefits, which their deceased husbands often attempted to provide in wills.

Ruth Baker received the use of the "Back room and Entry" of the plantation of her deceased husband; Elizabeth Snoad, the "two front room, & the three Front Chambers of . . . the Dwelling House." William Barrow and Patrick Maule directed their executors to build houses for their widows. Barrow also willed his plantation to his wife during "her natural life," and Henry Baker and Caleb Callaway devised half their plantations and orchards to their wives during their widowhood.

In its various manifestations the family proved to be the linchpin of colonial society. It was a key to orderly settlement, the conduit of cultural transmission, the seat of education and religion, and the center of much of the economic activity in the colony. Although subject to various pressures that threatened its integrity and altered its structure over time, the family endured as the most viable element of society in North Carolina and early America.

CHAPTER THREE

# SERVITUDE AND SLAVERY

The enormity of the geographic expanse of the New World required vast numbers of people to render the land remunerative. Europeans who immigrated to America and North Carolina enhanced their economic potential by resorting to bonded labor, principally indentured servitude and African slavery. Although servants and slaves represented forced labor, they also constituted a steady stream of immigrants that accelerated population growth in the colonies.

The institution of indentured servitude encompassed sundry forms of bound service. Indentured servants were primarily European immigrants who sold their labor for a stipulated number of years to defray their transportation expenses to America. Occasionally servitude was imposed upon criminals and vagrants in the provinces. The term derived from the contracts between laborers and masters or mistresses that were written in duplicate on large sheets of paper and divided along serrated or indented lines. The terminability of their contracts and the possession of civil rights distinguished servants from slaves.

Most servants entered into contracts in Europe, but others, called redemptioners, arrived in America without indentures. Upon their arrival arrangements were made for them. The contract or indenture contained the number of years of service for which the servant was obligated. The length of the term depended upon the amount of money needed by the servant but averaged three to five years. In return for control of the servant's labor, the master agreed to furnish adequate food, clothing, and lodging. At the end of the indenture, the master owed "freedom dues" to the servant to assist the servant in starting anew in life.

Indentured servants in North Carolina came from all parts of the British Isles. Most were young, and men predominated. While the majority signed indentures of their own volition, some may have been criminals who had been shipped to America at the order of the British government. Whereas servants were desired primarily as laborers and domestic help early in the colonial period, Carolinians sought skilled individuals during the Revolutionary era. Newspaper advertisements in the 1770s for runaway servants revealed, among others, two whitesmiths, two tailors, a bricklayer, a cabinetmaker, a currier, a sawyer, and a groom.

North Carolina statutes in 1715 and 1741 regulated servitude and slavery in the province, including the determination of the length of service for those servants arriving in the province without indentures. The 1715 law declared that servants over sixteen years of age should serve five years and that those under sixteen should serve until age twenty-two. Legislation in 1741, repealing the earlier law, fixed no specific period of service for those who immigrated without indentures and left all disputes to the county courts. The colonials apparently adhered broadly to the directive of the earlier law by contracting with servants after 1741 for five years of labor. Children served until they attained their legal majority.

The indenture, merely a piece of paper, was often difficult to retain. Lost, stolen, or destroyed contracts frequently occasioned disputes between servants and masters. Matters would have been easier had all purchasers of labor followed the example of Thomas Lovick, who registered his indenture in the Carteret County court and brought his servant to acknowledge publicly the obligation. Otherwise the county courts generally settled disputes over indentures.

Numerous cases involving servitude were heard by the courts. Michael Cain sought his freedom when his master, Thomas Thomson, lost his indenture, but the Rowan court directed Cain to serve his full term and an additional month to compensate Thomson for court fees and time lost from service while engaged in the legal proceedings. When Elizabeth Lawler complained about abusive treatment from

John Liddle, the Craven court told Liddle to produce the indenture by which he held the woman. Liddle admitted that he had none; Lawler confessed, however, that she had another sixteen months to serve. The court instructed her to remain with Liddle and demanded a bond from Liddle that he would pay lawful freedom dues to the servant and would not take her out of the province.

Unscrupulous persons sometimes attempted to secure servants by illegal indentures. In England James Phillips had boarded a ship in the Thames River as a cook. Upon arrival in North Carolina, he claimed that one Joseph Furden forced him to sign an indenture for five years service in the colony. In another case, Joshua Baker, the master of Snade Tedder, prevailed upon Richard Lewis to arrange a new indenture with Tedder before the servant's original term of indenture had expired. Under the arrangement Lewis would appear to be Tedder's new master but would assign Tedder back to Baker. The scheme was exposed, and the Carteret court freed Tedder from the second contract. The Craven court liberated Katherine Gale from New Bern schoolmaster John Green, Jonathan Hibbs, and others for "Confining Abusing and depriving her of Liberty," during which time she was forced to sign an indenture.

Many servants evidenced dissatisfaction with their confined lives by running away. They may have been inveigled or deceived into leaving Europe, suffered under brutal masters or mistresses, or sought adventure in the New World. In any case, by law runaway servants who were captured were required to serve double the time lost and additional time to compensate masters for costs accompanying apprehension.

Most runaways were males who obviously stood the best chance of traveling swiftly, gaining employment, and passing as free individuals. However, women also sought their freedom. Judith Williams left the service of James Briggs in 1745 but was quickly apprehended. Two years later she again departed, only to be caught in Virginia after an absence of four months. Mary Lambert, an Irish woman, described as having a very fresh complexion; beautiful long, black, curly hair; and a blemish in one eye, left the employ of newspaper publisher James Davis of New Bern in 1757.

Runaways were usually apprehended within one to eight weeks of their departure. If they eluded capture for more than two months, their chances of realizing permanent freedom were excellent. By that time the servants often were able to make their way out of the province, making identification and return more difficult. Nevertheless, some were caught after absences of one and even two years. After detention, servants would often attempt subsequent escapes. In Rowan in 1774, William Reed was sentenced to serve Thomas Lytle three months for time lost in running away. Subsequently Reed's contract was sold to Peter Short. The change little benefited the servant who was brought to court within a year and given an additional six months for leaving his new master.

The decision of some servants to run away was dictated by maltreatment, perhaps the deprivation of food and clothing or the imposition of undue punishment. The petition of Paul LeDuc prompted the Bertie court to order Dr. John Jameson to give his servant a half pound of meat and a pound and a half of bread each day. When Moses Gomez in New Hanover was accused of "not allowing [his servant] sufficient meat to eat with his bread kind," the court ordered him to treat his servant better and to provide him with the usual allowance of meat. The Craven justices instructed William Nicholson to allow his servant sufficient meat and drink, and to give him two shirts, a pair of stockings, and a pair of shoes.

Of course, not all complainants had legitimate grievances. Mary Coogan contended that Richard Lovett and his wife had unjustly beaten her and deprived her of clothes and other necessities. After listening to the allegations of both parties and viewing the servant regarding the beating, the Craven court decided that she had not been unduly corrected and ordered her back to her master. Another instance of alleged mistreatment involved Walterman Gibbs, who complained that his master, James Salter, had used him "ill by blows of Mitts sticks fire Tongs & back Swords." The Carteret justices were unimpressed and returned Gibbs to the service of Salter.

When servants brought legitimate protests of physical abuse or undue chastisement to the courts, the justices responded in various ways. In the case of Joseph Wakefield, a servant, the Chowan court decided that when Wakefield "shall deserve Correction[,] the sd. Holladay [master] shall apply himself to a Magistrate for the same." Onslow justices ordered Mabel Ryley's master not to correct her for trivial offenses but only for such as were deemed "culpable" by the nearest justice of the peace. In the case of Elinor McCome, the Cumberland court decided to require her master to post a bond for his proper behavior toward the servant.

More extreme measures were needed when masters continually failed to exercise self-restraint when correcting their servants. In January 1732, Dr. George Allen gave bond to the Chowan court that he would not exceed the bounds of moderation when punishing Matilda Sheriff. Six months later Allen was brought to court for abusing the servant, and the justices determined to sell Sheriff's contract for the time remaining on her indenture. After deducting the charges of the court, the proceeds were paid to Allen. The Onslow court treated John McGlothlin, servant of Thomas Jernegan, in similar fashion. After hearing several witnesses, the justices concluded that McGlothlin's "master has used him Extremely Ill" and ordered the servant sold for the remainder of his service.

Complaints by masters of absenteeism on the part of servants were matched in number only by cases involving illegitimate children born to servant women. Female servants paid a harsh penalty for their indiscretions and for unwanted attention forced on them. Before 1715 provincial law required women to serve an additional year for each illegitimate child born to them in order to compensate masters for the loss of time and work during pregnancy and childbirth. Legislation in 1715 increased the additional term of servitude to two years and subjected the servant to the prevailing fine for fornication. In 1741 the penalty was reduced to one year. The courts generally meted out sentences according to the dictates of the law, though the Craven justices deemed six months additional service sufficient for Mary O'Hara in 1757.

Often women involved in bastardy cases appeared in court on more than one occasion for a variety of reasons. Moll Sullivan, servant of Charles Cogdell, was brought to court in 1728 for giving birth to an illegitimate child and was ordered to serve an extra two years for the offense. By 1735 she was serving Samuel Noble and had run away from him. Her absence added seven months to her term of servitude. Ann Faughy had an illegitimate child in the service of Abraham Mitchell, who paid her fine and received the customary two years of additional service. Apparently Mitchell was not satisfied with the judgment of the court because six months later Ann Faughy complained of "immoderate correction" at the hands of her master.

Several servant women gave birth to more than one child. Charlotte D'Armand in Rowan County bore at least five children. Many times the children in question were mulattoes. Although some of the interracial liaisons may have been fleeting amours, in Carteret County Christian Finny's relations with a slave belonging to Cary Godbe threatened to detain her in permanent servitude. Finny bore at least three mulatto children within eight years, prolonging her servitude accordingly.

Freedom dues were another issue of disagreement between servants and masters. Most indentures signed in England and those executed in America specified that freedom dues were to be given at the end of the indenture according to the laws of the province. In the seventeenth century such dues consisted of a fifty-acre headright grant to each servant, but by 1705 they had been changed to Indian corn and wearing apparel. Legislation in 1715 denominated freedom dues as three barrels of Indian corn and two new suits of clothes or, alternatively for men, corn, one suit of clothes, and a gun. The 1741 law altered the dues to a sum of money and a suit of clothes.

Petitions for freedom dues evidenced one of the outstanding grievances of servants. All too frequently they had to resort to the courts to obtain compensation from masters. The justices almost always sympathized with the servants. Yet, despite court directives, restitution by masters was not always immediately forthcoming. Moses Arnal first petitioned the Tyrrell court in September 1752. The case was referred to the next court, continued in December 1752, and settled finally in June 1753. Rachel Smith, servant of Elizabeth Bell, waited even longer for her freedom dues. She petitioned the Tyrrell court in September 1735. In March 1737 she informed the court that Bell had not paid the freedom dues, and in June 1737 the justices ordered the provost marshal to levy the dues by distraint.

For North Carolina, and for the provinces in general, indentured servitude brought colonists to America and helped to meet the incessant demand for labor. However, crime increased in the wake of the importation of criminals and malcontents from England. Immorality was encouraged by the predicament of large numbers of young people who could not marry without consent and by the compromised situation of women in servitude. Finally, the expense of obtaining and supporting servants, plus the hardening attitudes toward humans engendered by this form of restricted servitude, helped prepare the way for slavery, which became prominent in North Carolina after 1750.

The slave code of the colony emanated principally from laws passed in 1715 and 1741, which were supplemented and modified by less significant statutes. The 1715 legislation represented a duplication or slight alteration of earlier enactments, which in turn reflected the influence of Virginia laws. The statute attempted to minimize the independence and mobility of slaves, discourage commercial and social relations between slaves and whites, and reduce the possibility of slave runaways and violence. The 1741 statute reiterated many of the provisions of the earlier law but, representing in part a reaction to the 1739 Stono Rebellion in South Carolina, proved more punitive than the 1715 law.

The fragments of evidence concerning the condition of slaves in North Carolina reveal a pattern of life similar to that in other southern colonies. However, if the keen observations of Massachusetts visitor Josiah Quincy Jr. are accepted, North Carolinians accorded their slaves better treatment than did South Carolinians (and probably Virginians). Smaller agricultural units and small average slaveholdings resulted in less demanding work and more personal concern for slaves. Hence, according to Quincy, North Carolina slaves were "better clothed and better fed, . . . and are of consequence better servants."

Other observers agreed that the slaves were not overworked. William Byrd found North Carolinians incorrigibly indolent and noted that slaves and freemen alike observed Sunday seven days a week. Of course, Byrd's hyperbole must be discounted. Still, Ebenezer Hazard found that slaves in North Carolina enjoyed their customary Sunday holiday, and a contemporary Scotsman stated that North Carolinians treated their "servants in an indulgent manner and something like rational beings." Field work was accomplished by the task as opposed to the gang system, which allowed slaves considerable free time in the afternoons. They utilized that advantage to hunt and trap animals and to cultivate patches of land allotted them by their masters for raising rice, corn, potatoes, tobacco, poultry, and livestock. Janet Schaw, visiting the Lower Cape Fear on the eve of the

Revolution, felt that many slaves were better fed and nourished than the poor whites of the colony.

The produce that the slaves did not need could be legally bartered or sold to their masters. Nevertheless, slaves often ignored the legal strictures in order to find a more lucrative trade with other whites. Thomas Clifford Howe and William Hooper complained publicly about whites who were willing to purchase goods that their slaves had purloined. Howe warned the populace around New Bern not to deal with his blacks unless the slaves could produce a "Certificate, signed by Me," giving them permission to sell their wares. Hooper, troubled by thievery at his plantation and his town house in Wilmington, promised to prosecute "with the utmost rigour" whites who bought from his slaves.

Masters expended little on the maintenance of slaves. The wearing apparel distributed to slaves generally confirmed William Attmore's observation that "clothes are not bestowed on [them] with much profusion." Occasionally slaves received allotments of osnaburg or Negro cloth, a pair of shoes, and a Dutch blanket, but these articles were expected to last a year or more. Of course, some fared better than others. Ben and Chloe, two young slaves who belonged to orphan Hardie Maund of Edgecombe County, usually received shoes and a blanket each year; in addition, there were pants, coat, and jacket for Ben and shifts and jackets for Chloe.

The diet of slaves was as meager as their clothing, unless they belonged to masters who permitted them to tend garden plots. Otherwise, they existed on corn products. Only the most lenient masters granted an allowance of meat. The fare could worsen on plantations supervised by overseers for absentee owners. Penelope Dawson wrote that one of her slaves "came to me yesterday morning with a grevious [sic] complaint of being starved, & that he was sure the Negroes would leave the plantation if there was not an alteration made." She knew that corn was scarce but felt that the overseer might "be too saving of the wheat."

The minimal support accorded slaves helped to make them a planter's most valuable possession. Recognizing the value of slaves, the colony attempted to protect such property by numerous laws designed to prevent or curtail the distraint of bondsmen for taxes, quitrents, and debts. When granting stipends to widows of militiamen killed in the

Battle of Alamance in 1771, the assembly attested to the value of bondsmen by directing that the money be placed in trust and used only for the purchase of slaves. The continually increasing prices commanded by slaves also reflected the desirability of that form of labor.

The ease with which slaves were hired out also confirmed their valuable stature. A survey of guardian accounts in Edgecombe County between 1764 and 1778 produced only one instance of a slave who could not be hired out. The slave was a young woman who had given birth to a child; the following year, however, she and the child were hired for a nominal amount. Slaves were hired for periods varying from a week to multiples of a year. Usually the transactions were private, but Mary Gordon of New Bern announced that she would offer her slaves for hire at public auction if not soon approached with an offer.

The lives of slaves were regulated by the slave code, which demanded strict segregation of the races and curtailed any measure of independence possessed by slaves. In order to discourage runaways, provincial legislation required slaves to obtain passes before venturing beyond the bounds of their plantations. Other attempts to restrict slaves included the progressive curtailment of their hunting privileges. After 1729 slaves could hunt only on their master's lands except when accompanied by whites. Legislation in 1741 forbade slaves to hunt with any weapon, unless their masters first obtained a license for that purpose from the county court. By 1766 the slave's hunting range was limited to a five-mile radius around his master's house.

Of course, slaves easily and often evaded these legal restrictions. In the towns as well as in the countryside, slaves seemed to possess a considerable measure of freedom. Although North Carolina did not contain metropolises comparable to those in the northern colonies or to Charleston, South Carolina, there were towns of sufficient size to warrant a distinctly urban life-style. In these towns, particularly the larger ones of Edenton, New Bern, and Wilmington, slaves enjoyed a perceptible degree of liberty. This freedom at times bordered on an almost independent existence, much to the consternation of whites, who attempted unsuccessfully to control blacks.

The continuing effort to constrain slaves, particularly as the number of blacks in the colony increased, resulted in impediments to emancipation. The 1715 law allowed manumission for honest and faithful service but required that liberated slaves leave the province within six months. When freed, blacks sometimes circumvented the statute by leaving the province and subsequently returning for permanent residence. Legislation in 1723 prohibited freed blacks from returning to the colony under penalty of being sold into slavery for seven years. The statute of 1741 still permitted liberation but only for meritorious service, and slave owners contemplating manumissions were required first to obtain the approbation of their respective county courts.

North Carolinians seldom liberated their slaves because they represented a large investment whose value increased throughout the colonial era. Most manumissions occurred through wills, though some owners freed their slaves by deed, as did Benjamin Reed of Tyrrell County in 1756, who set his "Negro Quomons free from me . . . for Ever or from the Lawful Clame of any person or persons whatsoever. . . ." The circumstances of manumission by will varied widely. John Hecklefield freed "Jane, for her diligent care had of me in my Sickness." Jean Corbin liberated her "old Negroe fellow Peter, who hath Long & faithfully Served me," and she provided an annual annuity for him.

As a group, only the Quakers began to pursue a concerted antislavery program before the Revolution. In April 1774 the Standing Committee of the North Carolina Yearly Meeting adopted a policy whereby Quakers at their discretion might manumit their slaves. Eighteen months later the Yearly Meeting ordered that "no Friend in unity shall either buy or sell a Negroe without the Consent of [his] Monthly Meeting." In 1776 the Yearly Meeting decided that "Keeping our fellow men in Bondage is inconsistent with the Law of righteousness" and instructed those who held slaves to free them as soon as possible.

Nonetheless, despite the benefits of some freedom of action and occasional manumission, slaves remained chattels, and nowhere was this more obvious than in the hire and sale of bondsmen. As Johann Schoepf declared, "One cannot without pity and sympathy see these poor creatures exposed on a raised platform, to be carefully examined and felt by buyers." Samuel Johnston purchased three old slaves from the estate of a friend because they implored him "with tears streaming from their Eyes not to let them fall into the hands of strangers."

Slaves proved refractory in their bondage and expressed their discontent in ways that ranged from feigned illness and sabotage to physical violence and running away. Whites early manifested an anxiety about their slaves. In 1684 John Burnby notified the Albemarle County court that "he goes in Danger of his Life for feare of one Andrew a Negroe belonging to Mr. John Culpepper," and two years later a slave in the same county was executed for murdering his master.

Slave resistance was particularly threatening in the instances of poisoning and arson. Poisoning proved to be a recurring crime in the colony. A knowledge of plants and their powers, derived from Africa and perpetuated in America, provided slaves with a subtle means of retaliating against their masters. In Bertie County in 1769 a slave was charged with giving poison to another bondsman who intended to administer the substance to his overseer and master.

The threat of fire was also real indeed. Wooden structures blazed rapidly, and arson was difficult to prove. In Rowan County, Toney, a slave belonging to Walter Sharp, was accused of burning his master's house. Toney defiantly admitted "in plain and manifest Terms That he . . . did set fire to, and burn the Dwelling house" of Sharp. When asked if there was any reason why he should not be sentenced to death, the slave answered that he had none. Execution by hanging followed this admission. Toney's action exemplified an "inward-directed rebelliousness" against the slave system, which was self-defeating and even self-destructive in its results. Rather than run away, Toney wreaked his vengeance openly and proudly.

Most slaves who were unable or unwilling to endure their bondage ran away. Some departed for brief periods of time for respites from their harsh lives, after which they returned. These truants had no intention of leaving permanently or attempting to change their status. They remained close to the plantation or their quarters, but were sufficiently clever and resourceful to evade capture until ready to return.

Other runaways sought permanent freedom. In eastern North Carolina the many lowlands and swamps, particularly Dismal Swamp, provided ready havens. J. F. D. Smyth noted that these areas harbored "prodigious multitudes of every kind of wild beasts peculiar to America, as well as run-away Negroes, who in these horrible swamps are perfectly safe, and with the greatest facility elude the most diligent search of their pursuers." Slaves were known to have resided in such regions for as

Runaway slaves in the eastern part of the colony often sought refuge in the swamps of that area. The inaccessibility afforded by the swamps resulted in permanent freedom for some of the slaves. Picture from *Harper's New Monthly Magazine*, April 1866.

many as twenty to thirty years, erecting huts upon the patches of high ground, clearing small fields, and raising corn, hogs, and fowl.

Most runaways seeking permanent freedom were American-born blacks who had acquired a facility for the English language, possessed a ready skill, had been exposed extensively to white society, and were accustomed to dealing with whites. They usually ran off alone. Often the departures were carefully planned. Thomas Boman, a blacksmith who could read, write, and cipher, took cash, a horse with saddle and bridle, a pair of money scales, and three coats and a jacket, among other clothes.

A small minority of the runaways was born in Africa. They were either longtime residents of the colony and relatively well acculturated or new arrivals who immediately sought their freedom. Often they ran away in groups. Robert Williams advertised the apprehension of "two new Negroes" who were unable to make themselves understood, and the sheriff of Onslow County in 1769 notified the public of the capture of four recently imported slaves. Edward Batchelor and Company in New Bern advertised in January 1775 the sale of a number of newly arrived blacks. They spoke no English and must have been unfamiliar with the country. Yet the urge for freedom was too strong to resist. The next month Batchelor offered a reward for the capture of five of the slaves who had absconded. Batchelor believed that some unprincipled person "of a fairer Complexion, but darker Disposition than theirs" had enticed them to leave.

Masters whose runaways remained free and proved particularly destructive could have them outlawed. Outlawry was a legal process whereby slaves were placed beyond the law and their deaths encouraged. A declaration of outlawry was obtained from any two justices of the peace and permitted anyone to apprehend the runaways by any possible means. Masters often provided rewards that were substantially higher if the slaves were returned dead rather than alive. If death resulted, the killer was not subject to legal punishment, and the colony reimbursed the owner for the value of the slave.

The desperation of outlawed slaves and their penchant for self-destruction can be seen in the many cases in which they refused to be taken alive. Several committed suicide while fleeing their captors or after apprehension. Cudjo jumped off the bridge (probably Benjamin Heron's drawbridge) over the Northeast Cape Fear River and drowned. London and Belinda in New Hanover, and York in Craven also drowned while eluding their pursuers. Many slaves, not all of them outlawed, were also found dead in jail following capture in circumstances that strongly suggested suicide.

Any discussion of slave violence and runaways invariably settled on the most threatening form of discontent—conspiracy and insurrection. Whites viewed with suspicion any gathering of slaves. Early in the eighteenth century slaves were forbidden to construct meeting-houses for religious worship. Later slaves were prohibited from traveling at night and meeting in numbers in kitchens belonging to their masters or in their own quarters. By 1741, with the Stono Rebellion in South Carolina fresh in memory, legislators referred specifically to the problem of conspiracy when they declared that if three or more slaves shall meet to "consult, advise or conspire to rebel, or make insurrection, or shall plot or conspire the Murther of any Person," upon conviction they "shall suffer Death."

New Bern, February 20, 1775.

# ONE HUNDRED AND TEN POUNDS REWARD.

ABSENTED themselves very early on Sunday Morning the 19th Instant, from the House of the Subscribers, Five newly imported Slaves, (Four Men and One Woman:) Two of the Men, named *Kauchee* and *Boohum*, are Six Feet One or Two Inches high, and about 30 Years of Age; another named *Ji*, is near Five Feet Nine Inches high, and about 25 Years of Age, has sore Eyes; and the Fourth, named *Sambo Pool*, is a short well set Fellow, aged 18 Years; the Woman, named *Pig Minny*, is of short Stature and elderly. The Fellows were uniformly clad in coarse green Cloth Jackets, brown Cloth Trowsers, a Blanket, and red Cloth Cap; and the Wench had on an emboss'd Flannel Petticoat and brown Cloth Cloak. As they are incapable of uttering a Word of *English*, have been extremely well fed, and very little worked, it is surmised they have been inveigled away by some infamously principled Person, of a fairer Complexion, but darker Disposition than theirs. Whoever, therefore, secures the said Negroes for their Owners, and the Person or Persons so inveigling them, or facilitating their Escape, provided that he or they be convicted thereof, shall receive the above-mentioned Reward of *One Hundred and Ten Pounds*, Proclamation Money, or Forty Shillings for each of the Slaves.

## EDWARD BATCHELOR & Co.

**\*\*\*** All Masters of Vessels, Boatmen, and others plying by Water, are forbid to give them Passage at their Peril.

Slave owners often offered rewards for the capture and return of runaway slaves. Edward Batchelor's announcement of a reward for the return of five escaped slaves appeared in the *North Carolina Gazette* (New Bern) on February 24, 1775.

The threat, real or imagined, posed by armed slaves prompted the assembly in 1753 to institute the search or patrol system. Justices of the county courts were permitted to divide their counties into districts and appoint searchers or patrollers to examine black habitations at least four times a year for guns, swords, and other weapons. Most eastern and central counties utilized the patrol system. Searchers also walked the streets of Edenton, New Bern, Tarboro, and Wilmington. Nevertheless, many counties and towns found that the patrollers were negligent in their duties.

The onset of the Revolution brought what was perceived as the greatest threat of slave insurrection in the colony. Although the "Ethiopian Regiment" of Virginia governor Lord Dunmore was the most spectacular attempt by British authorities to use slaves to quell the colonial revolt, the Virginia example was somewhat paralleled by Governor Josiah Martin's veiled threat to use slaves to preserve order in North Carolina.

Events of early July 1775 convinced the colonials of the seriousness of Martin's implied threat. Whether prompted by rumors of Martin's call or by a desire to emulate the attempt of some provincials to seek independence from Great Britain, slaves in the eastern counties of Pitt, Martin, Beaufort, and Craven apparently contemplated organized insurrection with the intention of gaining their freedom. Although whites, suffering from mounting anxieties, probably exaggerated the menace, some concerted actions may have been planned by the slaves, but no insurrection occurred.

Slavery in colonial North Carolina, then, was a harsh institution, though perhaps not as severe as in Virginia or South Carolina. As the number of slaves in the colony increased, so did their attempts to improve their condition. At the same time, and reciprocally, whites exerted increasingly strenuous efforts to define a very subordinate status for slaves and relegate them to that position. Anxieties mounted on both sides, particularly since slaves persisted in activities that not only aimed to improve their circumstances but also covertly and openly attacked the repressive society in which they lived. Motivated by the desire for personal gain or suffused with apathy, some whites undermined the slave code and failed to take advantage of surveillance measures, such as the patrol, to attempt to control the slave population. This leniency and the slaves' continuous quest for liberty produced the potential for the most dangerous form of slave resistance, insurrection. The threat of insurrection during the colonial period reached its peak with the outbreak of the Revolution.

CHAPTER FOUR

# HOMES AND FURNISHINGS

As immigrants entered North Carolina, first from Virginia and then from more northerly colonies, South Carolina, and overseas, they faced the daunting tasks of starting a new life, planting crops, and erecting homes in a wilderness. Many factors influenced their manner of building: geographic location, climatic conditions, prevailing architectural styles, wealth of the owner, and the builder's expertise. A heavily wooded landscape compelled an early reliance on timber for building material. In the humid climate along the coast, open porches reflected the influence of the West Indies. A shortage of skilled labor, the high cost of nails and glass, and a frontier environment resulted in plain, if not crude, dwellings at the outset. The eventual accumulation of wealth by some, however, led to more impressive homes. Overall, great diversity characterized the construction of houses in North Carolina.

The first homes erected in the colony failed to survive. The early settlers built "earthfast" or "impermanent" structures whose framing members either rested on the ground or were attached to posts placed in the ground. As a result, the dwellings deteriorated or rotted, necessitating repairs or replacement perhaps within a decade. However, Carolinians found earthfast homes highly suitable, for they necessarily built in haste, lacked funds for more imposing houses, usually intended to move soon, and hoped to improve their fortunes and consequently their homes. Only when the colonials placed their

Log houses were common in the newly settled areas of the colony. The Allen House, located at the Alamance Battleground State Historic Site in Alamance County, is an example of eighteenth-century log construction. Photograph from the files of the Division of Archives and History.

structures on brick or stone foundations did they survive for long periods of time.

In the beginning many settlers resorted to log cabins. Most houses were one-room buildings with lofts and sheds or lean-tos for additional space. Popular variations included the double cabin, or two cabins under one roof. The saddlebag plan attached two buildings to either side of a single chimney. The dog-run plan separated two cabins by an open breezeway, which permitted ventilation, storage, and protected play. William Byrd, while surveying the boundary between Virginia and North Carolina in 1728, observed that many of the houses he saw were constructed of logs mortised together and covered with pine or cypress shingles. Doors swung on wooden hinges and were secured by wooden locks. Thus neither nails nor any other ironwork was necessary.

Among the poorer element of society, and particularly in the newly settled regions of the colony, log construction continued to be the norm

Slave cabins were usually simple dwellings with dirt floors and few furnishings. Typically the houses were clustered in one area of a plantation. Though this rendering of slave quarters appeared in *Harper's New Monthly Magazine* in November 1859, the crude cabins had changed little since the colonial era.

throughout the eighteenth century. Slaves were also relegated to crude, minimal habitations, if they did not reside in household kitchens, barns, or other outbuildings. Slave quarters were mainly cabins, poorly chinked, with dirt floors. Though excessively ventilated, and thereby cold during the winter, the cabins were dark, smoky, and usually crowded. Furnishings were few and often made by the slaves themselves.

The advent of a more settled society and the accumulation of wealth brought a transition from log to frame and brick construction. Material success was reflected not simply by larger structures but by such refinements as window glass, hardware, plastered walls, planed or paneled woodwork, and brick chimneys. However, many well-to-do built very conservatively. Janet Schaw visited a wealthy planter in the Lower Cape Fear whose house, she thought, was hardly better than his slave cabins. This humble approach to building by the wealthy represented the leveling spirit in North Carolina as well as the fear that ostentation might antagonize social inferiors and jeopardize oligarchic control.

Light frame houses eventually came to dominate home construction in the colony. Most were modest, but some that survive are impressive. The Cupola House in Edenton, built in 1758 and noted for its octagonal dome and overhanging second story, is a fine example of the lingering impact of Jacobean architecture. In Bath the Palmer-Marsh House, dating from 1751, is a large frame structure, twenty-five by fifty-one feet with two stories and an attic, that represents the subsequent Georgian style. The Burgwin-Wright House in Wilmington, constructed about 1771 by wealthy merchant and planter John Burgwin, also evidences the Georgian form. The house is marked by a double slope roof, double porches front and back, a central stair passage, and a principal room located on the second floor.

In the Piedmont, German architecture, particularly that of the Moravians, contrasted sharply with the prevalent British mode of building. The Moravians preferred masonry construction, but in the backcountry, where lime for mortar was difficult to obtain, they resorted to *fachwerk*, or timber framing infilled with brick and sometimes plastered, which was common in Germany and much of northern Europe. The Single Brothers House in (Old) Salem, a fifty-by-thirty-eight-foot *fachwerk* structure erected in 1768-1769, reflects the superb craftsmanship of the Moravians. Together with other buildings that lined the streets of Salem, the Single Brothers House gave the town a very distinctive look, almost medieval in nature, compared to the British towns elsewhere in North Carolina.

Brick houses exemplified wealth and conveyed a sense of power and permanence, if not elegance. The mortar often contained pieces of shell since the colonials made their lime from oyster and other shells. The Newbold-White House in Perquimans County, a brick structure that dates from 1730, reveals impressive decorative detail and superb brickwork. The most eminent example of colonial brick construction is Tryon Palace in New Bern, finished in 1770 as a gubernatorial residence and statehouse. A fire in 1798 destroyed two of the three principal buildings in the Palace complex, but in the mid-twentieth century the structures were rebuilt, the remainder was refurbished, and the Palace and grounds were opened as a historic site.

In the Piedmont, colonials occasionally used stone for building purposes. The Braun House near Salisbury in Rowan County, finished

Tryon Palace in New Bern was designed and built by English architect John Hawks as the official residence of North Carolina's colonial governor. The structure was completed in 1770 and occupied by Gov. William Tryon. In 1798 two of the main buildings were devastated by fire. They were rebuilt in the mid-twentieth century, and today Tryon Palace is open to the public as a state historic site. Photograph from the files of the Division of Archives and History.

in 1766 and the best surviving example of Germanic architecture outside of Salem, is a massive two-story structure with walls two feet thick. The Alexander House, finished in 1774 and now in Charlotte, is another example of the use of rock in a similarly powerful, imposing home that reflects fine workmanship and the wealth of its owner.

Although the simple one-room log cabins and rudimentary frame houses remained common, other floor plans were used. The hall-and-parlor arrangement, mainly of English and Scotch-Irish origin, consisted of a large living room-kitchen combination (hall) and a small, private bedroom (parlor). The two-story, three-room Continental or Quaker plan brought by the Germans to the Piedmont was more elaborate. By the 1760s and 1770s some builders began to use central passages or hallways, producing the "I" house, perhaps the most common folk dwelling in the eastern part of the country. Lofts or at-

Stone was occasionally used for building in the Piedmont. The Michael Braun House (above) was completed in 1766 near Salisbury. Braun, a native of Germany, was a wealthy political and business leader in Rowan County. The Hezekiah Alexander House was finished in 1774 and is located in Mecklenburg County. Alexander, a Maryland native, was a prominent citizen of the county and a local leader in the Presbyterian Church. Photographs from the files of the Division of Archives and History.

tics were included in many designs and served as bedrooms and storage areas.

Other features of colonial homes varied as widely as the building materials and floor plans. Gabled roofs usually topped the houses, though the gambrel, which offered more space above stairs under the roof, and the hipped, used mainly for outbuildings, became increasingly popular in the eighteenth century. Sheds and porches, often later enclosed or partially enclosed, provided more room in houses that were ordinarily small and crowded.

Porches were a critical element of early houses, joining home interiors with the exterior environment. Although porches might be added to buildings already finished, after about 1740 they began to be integrated into the original structures. The broad, functional sitting porches, also variously called galleries, verandas, and piazzas, were found along the coast from the Lower Cape Fear to Edenton. These porches bore witness to the influence of the West Indies, with which North Carolina conducted a substantial trade. Just north of Brunswick Town was Russellborough, an elegant house well described by one of its occupants, Lieutenant Governor William Tryon, who noted that "there is a Piaza [that] Runs Round the House both Stories of ten feet Wide with a Ballustrate of four Feet high, which is a great Security for my little girl."

Numerous outbuildings surrounded many of the houses. In the more primitive dwellings cooking was done in the house, while in some of the more elaborate homes the kitchen was in the cellar. Often, however, kitchens were detached from the houses, in part because of the danger of fire. The range of additional outbuildings included well houses, smokehouses, dairies, coach houses, privies, and barns.

Ornamental gardens complemented the homes of the wealthy who could afford the leisure and expense of such luxuries. Gardens not only represented beauty to those who appreciated the aesthetics of nature, but were also an attempt to imitate the contemporary European gentry and thus secure corresponding social prominence in America. John Burgwin maintained gardens covering three acres at the Hermitage, his plantation north of Wilmington. A creek wound through the largest garden. A fishpond was linked to the creek, and both contained an abundance of fish. The garden contained several alcoves, summerhouses, and a hothouse, as well as the family chapel.

There was also a second ornamental garden and the vegetable or "cook's" garden.

In terms of size and value, beds, other large furniture, and kitchen utensils constituted the bulk of the furnishings in the average colonial household. Feather beds were the most popular items and represented an element of wealth in the home. Flock beds—mattresses stuffed with woolen or cotton refuse, rags, corn husks, or other material—were less desirable alternatives. Cradles and trundle beds were used for children, with the trundle beds neatly slipped under the larger beds in the day and brought out for use at night.

Colonials used the word "bed" to describe the mattress. The bedsteads and bed "furniture" were separate items. Bedsteads were wooden frames with a cord laced back and forth to support the mattress. The wealthy had elaborate headboards and four-poster bedsteads with hanging curtains surrounding the bed for warmth, protection, and privacy. The "furniture" accompanying the bed included such curtains, as well as pillows, sheets, blankets, rugs (bed rugs, heavier than blankets), coverlets, quilts, and comforters.

Other large furniture was kept to a minimum because the houses were generally small. Trunks and chests were tucked away in corners. Chests of drawers, safes, and cupboards also served for storage. The more commodious houses were furnished with varying numbers and styles of tables and chairs, leather couches, and desks of mahogany, walnut, maple, and pine.

In homes where the cooking was done in the house, the kitchen, with its huge fireplace, dominated the interior. Fire shovels, tongs, and one or more box irons and heaters, or warming pans, were placed beside the hearth. An enormous variety of cooking utensils cluttered the fireplace and its surroundings. Pothooks and racks hung at the mouth of the chimney, and andirons stood on the floor. Iron, brass, and copper kettles and pots rested nearby, accompanied by skillets, frying pans, saucepans, skimmers, ladles, and flesh forks. For use in the preparation of food, colanders, pattypans, hand mills, sifters, graters, and various items of woodenware were available.

Food was eaten in close proximity to the kitchen. Tables were used where available, and the wealthy owned fine tablecloths. The less affluent used cloths of simple materials or improvised. Most colonials possessed the usual complement of knives, forks, and spoons and ate

The fireplace in the kitchen at Tryon Palace is surrounded by the wide variety of utensils used in colonial cooking. Photograph from the files of the Division of Archives and History.

from dishes, plates, trenchers, and porringers, which were generally pewter but often wood or earthenware. Wealthy families sometimes owned fine silver and china. Bowls, tureens, cups, mugs, and tumblers—also made from diverse materials—served to hold liquids. Bottles of various kinds and sizes, pepperboxes, mustard pots, and butter pots were kept in the vicinity of the kitchen; saltcellars often served as centerpieces for colonial tables.

Wild and domesticated animals supplied a variety of meat and dairy products for the colonials. Deer and small game were especially plentiful. Large stocks of cattle provided beef for the colonial table. Hogs thrived to the extent that pork—salted or on the hoof—was one of the colony's principal exports and earned Carolinians the nickname "porkers." The colonials tended to let the cattle and hogs forage in the woods, however, thereby lowering the quality of meat derived from the animals. Most families also kept a number of sheep, though primarily for wool; North Carolinians were not as fond of mutton as the English. Goats were raised sparingly because they were not worth the trouble, and they played havoc with crops and gardens.

Domestic fowl added another dimension to the colonial diet. Geese, ducks, turkeys, and chickens abounded around the houses and barns. Feathers as well as meat and poultry products rendered these "dunghill fowl" valuable. Despite a favorable climate and an abundance of food, particularly corn, only a small percentage of barnyard fowl lived to maturity due to the mismanagement or neglect of the colonials. Still, North Carolina planters took pride in their reputation, whether true or not, of having the largest flocks of domestic poultry in the British Empire.

Along the coast and rivers people supplemented their diets with varieties of shellfish and finfish. Seafood, particularly oysters, was a staple in the meals of Beaufort residents. The provincials often fished in the inland waters, more for food than for pleasure. Travelers, commenting on the swarming of the rock bass at the falls of the Roanoke River near Halifax, said that a dog thrown into the water would not be able to swim to the other side due to the congestion of fish. This phenomenon was called the "rock fight," and men easily killed the fish with sticks. On the Roanoke and other rivers, mullet, trout, and perch prompted fishermen to stretch weirs or nets across the water to catch the fish. These nets so greatly interfered with navigation that the provincial assembly passed legislation to regulate that type of fishing.

Most colonials, rich and poor alike, maintained orchards from which they derived fruit and liquor. The principal fruits were apples and peaches, which were converted into huge quantities of brandy and cider. These fruits were so abundant that travelers passing an apple or peach orchard felt free to help themselves; the owners not only did not object but encouraged such license since the fruit was so plentiful that it was rarely sold. In fact, during season the colonials even fed apples and peaches to their hogs. Less common fruits included pears, apricots, cherries, quinces, and plums.

The drinking habits of Carolinians clearly indicated a propensity for alcoholic beverages. The colonials imported wines, rum, and malt liquors; they manufactured whiskey, brandy, and cider. During the colonial era distilling became a major industry in the province. However, only a minority of the people owned stills because the apparatus was very expensive. Such property was carefully preserved and bequeathed at a man's death to his wife or children that they might "still" their own liquor. The possession of less expensive apple mills was more widespread.

The consumption of liquor was not reserved for any age, sex, or class. Infants might drink cider and three-year-old children a glass of rum in the mornings to ward off "noxious vapors." Delicate women downed hard cider. And the colonials drank on every possible occasion. Weddings, funerals, ordinations, vestry meetings, musters, elections, court meetings, slave auctions, and house-raisings occasioned the outpouring of spirits. Such activities as musters and house-raisings were often subverted by the consumption of excessive quantities of rum or brandy.

The assortment of drinks consumed had various origins. Madeira seemed the most popular wine, followed by claret and red ports, probably from Great Britain. Wines were also imported from Teneriffe Island in the Canaries and from southern Europe. Rum came from the New England colonies and the West Indies. William Byrd found New England rum so bad that it was aptly called "Kill-Devil," a universal term applied to rum drink in seventeenth-century America. Imported beer originated primarily in Philadelphia and New York but occasionally arrived from Bristol, England. A variety of homemade beer was made from persimmons. Where apples and peaches were scarce, Carolinians picked ripe persimmons, combined them with wheat bran, and kneaded the mixture into loaves which were baked in ovens. From these was brewed a fermented liquor called persimmon beer, which had an acceptable taste. The colonials produced most of their brandy and cider in North Carolina, though French brandy was relished when it could be obtained. Occasionally brandy was distilled from potatoes, but it was a much less desirable drink.

Of course, the colonials mixed their drinks. Flips were warm or cold concoctions containing mostly strong beer sweetened with sugar or molasses and flavored with a "touch" of rum. Punches were universal and potent mixtures of tea, rum (arrack), sugar, lemons (or lemon juice), limes, or oranges, and water. Grog contained water with a fourth, fifth, or sixth part of rum. Toddies usually consisted of rum, water, and sugar, though occasionally brandy was substituted for the rum. Bumbo consisted of half rum and half water with sugar added.

This eighteenth-century tea caddy was used in Edenton. The colonists drank large quantities of tea, much of which was imported from Great Britain. Photograph from the files of the Division of Archives and History.

Wines, too, were used in mixtures. Wine, sugar, water, and a little nutmeg produced sangaree; wine, sugar, and fresh milk yielded syllabub.

Carolinians were not totally addicted to alcoholic beverages, however. They consumed large amounts of coffee, tea, and chocolate, particularly for breakfast. The colonials, most being British, drank much tea, which they imported from Great Britain. They also concocted their own brand of the drink from the yaupon bush or tree, a variety of the southern holly. Yaupon tea eventually complemented smuggled Dutch tea, which the colonials imported illegally after agreeing not to buy British tea in protest against the Townshend tea tax in 1767.

Meals varied according to the economic fortunes of the people. Among the wealthy they constituted one of the daily burdens of the mistress of the house who directed the activities of the household. It was she who supervised the poultry yard, dairy, and smokehouse, and it was she who determined the variety of dishes prepared for the meals. Of course, she was aided by a bevy of servants and guided in the preparation of dishes by directions from mother, advice of friends, and written treatises such as E. Smith's *The Compleat Housewife* and Martha Bradley's *The British Housewife*. Resulting dishes were often rich, well seasoned, and complicated. Tables fairly groaned under the offerings of meats, vegetables, pastries, and beverages. The always bountiful table of William Dry caused his residence just north of Brunswick to be known as the house of universal hospitality.

The meals of the wealthy were leisurely, luxurious affairs. The men of the gentry rose late in the morning and breakfasted between nine and ten o'clock on cold meats, fowl, hominy, bread and butter, and tea or coffee. Dinner, between two o'clock and half past four, constituted the principal meal of the day. One traveler reported having dined on fat roasted turkeys, geese, ducks, boiled fowls, large hams, hung beef, and barbecued pig. Vegetables and such pastries as minced pies, cheesecakes, tarts, and biscuits supplemented that repast. Gentlemen drank ciders, toddies, punches, and particularly wines. Toasts were profuse, as many as twenty to thirty being offered at a single meal. After a late afternoon tea, a light supper was eaten between eight and ten o'clock.

Lower- and middle-class individuals might rise about six in the morning, have a strong drink, work for two or three hours, and breakfast at nine or ten o'clock on a variety of cold meats, hominy, toast, bread and butter, tea, coffee, or chocolate, and cider. Dinner, enjoyed in midafternoon, consisted of the standing dishes of ham, pork, and greens, plus cider or brandy. Often these people omitted supper, instead sipping some alcoholic drink during the late evening.

The fare was not always desirable. William Logan's journey through North Carolina in 1745 included eating at one Chilly's house between Edenton and Bath where he had "some chickens broiled in a nasty manner" for his dinner. Before he reached New Bern he stopped at a house where he was "vilely entertained, having nothing but Potato Bread mixed with Indian Corn & rank Irish Butter." About fifteen miles north of Wilmington, Logan stopped at another house where the inhabitants had been subsisting for days on potatoes and some chickens. On the other hand, a French traveler in 1765 dined at a farmer's home on good fat bacon, greens, corn bread, and fine cider.

The slaves' diet was scanty and unwholesome. Upon rising at daybreak they received a small amount of hominy or hoecake and then worked until noon. At that time they might receive an hour's respite during which they ate their dinner of hominy with salt, perhaps flavored once or twice a week with a little fat, skimmed milk, bacon, or salt fish.

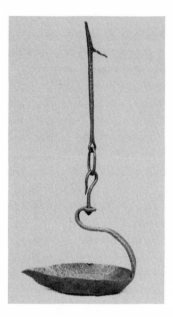

Betty lamps were a simple and popular source of light. Tallow, grease, and oil were used for fuel, resulting in a smoky, malodorous flame. Photograph from the files of the Division of Archives and History.

After dusk, if work lasted that long, the slaves consumed their last meal of the day, generally consisting of the same monotonous corn products. The more fortunate plantation slaves were permitted small gardens, which they tended in their spare moments on weekdays and on Sundays. The produce either supplemented their diets or was sold or exchanged for articles of clothing, pipes, and knives.

Candles and lamps provided illumination for meals and other household activities. Tallow made from every type of fat and grease was saved for candles. Wax candles were less common, though most farmers kept several beehives from which they derived wax as well as honey. Few Carolinians used the berries of the myrtle, which grew profusely along the coast. Plucking and boiling the berries several times for a few hours would have yielded excellent wax, but the people shied from the work involved.

Lamps were used less frequently. The earliest were various types of fat lamps; the most popular were the Betty lamps, which were small, shallow receptacles with projecting noses. They were filled with tallow, grease, or oil, and a piece of rag or coarse wick was laid on the nose. The Betty lamps produced a "dull, smoky, ill-smelling flame." Between 1785 and 1800 Betty lamps were replaced by more sophisticated pewter and glass lamps of various shapes and sizes.

Cards for straightening fibers and spinning wheels were common in colonial households. Photograph from the files of the Division of Archives and History.

In addition to candlemaking, another household manufacture was reflected in the numerous spinning wheels found in the colonial homes. Most households contained at least one linen wheel and one woolen wheel, plus sets of cards for straightening cotton and wool fibers. After carding, the fibers were spun into thread, which was used for weaving the family's cloth. Many colonials, however, depended upon weavers, tailors, or friends with looms to weave the thread into their "country-made" cloth. Bulky, expensive, and complicated looms were not standard household items, though they appeared more frequently toward the close of the colonial period. Girls were taught to knit at an early age, and knitted apparel formed an integral part of the family clothing.

The colonials were far from self-sufficient when clothing themselves. Tailor-made garments and finished articles of clothing sold by merchants were exceedingly popular. Since clothing often represented a considerable investment, the colonials selected their wardrobes carefully. The fabrics used in making clothes varied widely. Irish linen, particularly checked linen, always found a ready market. Holland, a glazed or unglazed cotton or linen, sold well. The most popular material was probably osnaburg, a coarse linen originally made in Osnabruck, Germany. Still, the list would not be complete without mentioning Belgian duffil (duffel), German serge, French lawn and cambric, Oriental calico, muslin, and Persian as well as fearnought, drugget, shalloon, frieze, chintz, buckram, durance, and dowlas, among many other materials.

Various types of clothing characterized colonial dress. The outermost garment for women was a gown, probably composed of a skirt, bodice, and sleeves that tied or buttoned to the bodice. One or more petticoats, sometimes designated as "top" and "under" petticoats, were worn under the gown, beneath which a loose linen shift served as the essential item of underclothing. To prevent undue soiling of the skirts, aprons were commonly worn. Neckcloths served a similar purpose for the bodice. Footwear included thread, silk, or worsted stockings, and leather, cloth, or silk shoes, sometimes accompanied by clogs, or half-slippers with wooden soles, to protect the shoes from mud and water. Caps, bonnets, and hats covered the head, while cloaks and hoods gave added warmth in cool weather. Gloves, often kid, were popular; handkerchiefs abounded.

The wardrobe of Mary Gainor of Edgecombe County might illustrate the clothing of a North Carolina woman in the colonial era. She owned 11 gowns, 5 petticoats, 5 shifts, 2 hats, 2 pairs of gloves, 2 pairs of stockings, 1 pair of shoes, and a "parcel" of caps, handkerchiefs, and aprons. The wife of Justice of the Peace Jesse Hare possessed 10 gowns, 9 petticoats, 3 riding coats, 2 cloaks, 2 fine aprons, 2 fine handkerchiefs, 5 caps, 1 hat, 1 pair of hose, and 2 pairs of shoes. These women and others enhanced their appearance with rings, bracelets, necklaces, lockets, earrings, and other jewelry. The daughter of Gov. Gabriel Johnston owned five gold lockets, a garnet necklace set in silver, a Bristol stone necklace set in silver, a gold watch and chain, a set of gold tweezers, a gold girdle buckle, and a Bristol stone girdle buckle set in silver.

William Gainor, husband of Mary, displayed an average variety and amount of clothing for a man. He possessed 1 coat, 3 jackets, 3 pairs of breeches, 2 shirts, 1 hat, and 2 caps. Vests and waistcoats were also common items of male attire, accompanied by coats and "greatcoats" when added protection or warmth was needed. Breeches ended slightly below the knee, although long breeches or trousers were common. Many planters favored leather breeches because of their durability. Silk, worsted, or thread stockings, supported by garters, covered the calf. Shoes and boots formed the preponderance of footwear, but pumps occasionally appeared.

Caps, including nightcaps, were commonly worn. Most men also owned at least one or two hats, which were generally made of felt or beaver. However, other furs, more expensive than beaver, were used for hat making. Constant Devotion, a hatter, left at his death not only 28 beaver skins and 33 beaver hats, but also 155 raccoon skins, 4 otter skins, and 5 muskrat skins.

Men also had many opportunities to display jewelry. Silver knee and shoe buckles were common. So were silver breeches buckles and clasps as well as ivory and gilt vest buttons. Gold and silver rings were popular, particularly mourning rings given by the family of a deceased person to close friends and relatives. Snuffboxes, elaborately adorned, and watches added glamour to the male attire.

Fashion-conscious women and men attempted to stay abreast of the latest styles of hair dress. The advertisement of James Verrier, peruke and hat maker in New Bern, announced that he dressed

ladies and gentlemen's hair in the newest and best approved fashion and [made] all sorts of ladies full dress toupees, [undress] toupees, plain rolls, beads pleats, and side curls, convenient for dress and undress, also all sorts of gentlemen's full dress bag and bob wigs, . . . false tails and curls, likewise spring curls for gentlemen whose side locks are thin or come off, so natural as not to be discovered by the most curious eye.

Wigs remained popular throughout the colonial era, but as the Revolution approached a preference for natural hair became evident.

Clothing for children closely resembled that of adults. Of course, the wearing apparel varied according to age and wealth. The more fortunate—that is, wealthy—boys received from two to five shirts a year, one or two pairs of breeches or trousers, perhaps a matching waistcoat and breeches, and probably a coat or jacket. Rapid growth of children necessitated at least one pair of shoes per year, which was often supplemented by a pair of boots. Occasionally a pair of yarn stockings accompanied the acquisition of shoes. The boys expected one hat per year, usually felt or beaver but sometimes raccoon.

The amount of clothing acquired yearly by girls has been more difficult to determine. Often cloth was purchased for the girls, as much as thirty yards a year, which the girls, their families, or tailors converted into finished items of clothing, such as gowns, petticoats, sacks, shifts, banyans, and jackets. Girls received a pair of gloves, handkerchiefs, and at least one pair of shoes and stockings annually. Caps and hats were also standard attire.

The clothing of the slaves was often minimal. Young children frequently ran about naked, while even the older slaves in some instances wore only a breechclout or petticoat. Nevertheless, records show that many masters afforded slaves better treatment. Advertisements for runaway slaves indicated that they were often well clothed. Richmond, who belonged to the company of Ancrum and Schaw in Wilmington, wore a white shirt, leather breeches, striped flannel jacket, and a pair of shoes and stockings at his departure. Many others were similarly clad in a diverse selection of clothes.

Despite the variety and even elegance of clothes, North Carolinians apparently took poor care of them. A traveler in the Cape Fear area in the 1770s found the people to be among the worst "clothes washers" that she had ever seen. All clothes, regardless of material or color, were thrown together in a copper or iron pot with boiling water and a piece of soap. After being turned over a few times with a stick, the clothes were removed, rinsed, squeezed, and put on pales to dry. Bleaching was disregarded. The same observer also noted that Cape Fear housewives shunned soapmaking. Although the quality of potash in the area was excellent, the women preferred to purchase soap at extravagant prices. And then they often received inferior Irish soap.

The colonials owned a myriad of personal items—from clocks to chamber pots to mousetraps—to bring a measure of comfort, convenience, and safety into their lives. A smooth face demanded a razor, hone, and looking glass; neatness necessitated brushes for hats, clothes, and shoes. Poor vision accounted for numerous pairs of spectacles. The minuteman concept of every colonial male ready to spring armed to a call of distress hardly applied to North Carolinians. Perhaps two-thirds of the men kept guns—pistols, double-barreled pistols, muskets, rifles, shotguns, and blunderbusses. Such accoutrements as powder horns, shot bags, shot, powder, flints, and cartouche boxes accompanied the guns. As many as one-fifth of the colonials also owned swords.

Men often worked in their homes and kept the tools of their occupations in their houses or in separate rooms or wings adjoining the buildings. The workbench of Thomas Hobgood, turner and joiner,

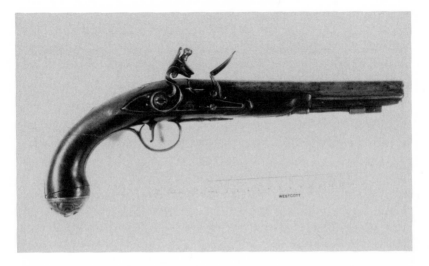

Weapons, such as this flintlock pistol, were common in North Carolina. As many as two-thirds of the men owned guns. Photograph from the files of the Division of Archives and History.

contained 4 gouges, 2 files, 2 augers, 9 chisels, 4 planes, 2 drawing knives, 4 plane irons, a tenant saw, handsaw, cooper's adz, froe, shaving knife, hammer, taper bit, gimlet, mandrel, compass, ruler, jointer, some brass nails, a glue pot, and "some other tools." Shoemakers, hatters, and physicians also worked inside their homes. Furthermore, men who were primarily planters generally kept a variety of tools, such as those of carpentry and shoemaking, needed for making the simple articles required by a family.

The clutter outside the house, under sheds or lean-tos and in barns or small outbuildings, was as great as that found inside. Saddles, bridles, and halters hung from the walls as did reap hooks, scythes, and pieces of rope. Horse collars and hames awaited use, while various tubs, pails, baskets, and casks occupied much space. Every man possessed an ax and hatchet in addition to a pair of iron wedges for splitting wood. Steelyards for weighing agricultural produce were a vital part of the household. Tools and implements, such as hoes, plows, flails, and brakes, reflected the cultivation of tobacco, corn, cotton, flax, wheat, and rice, among other crops. (Two other booklets published by the Division of Archives and History, N.C. Department of Cultural

Resources, describe the development of agriculture in North Carolina: Cornelius O. Cathey, *Agriculture in North Carolina Before the Civil War*; and Jerome E. Brooks, *Green Leaf and Gold: Tobacco in North Carolina*.)

CHAPTER FIVE

# HEALTH, EDUCATION, AND WELFARE

*Health*

America provided a common meeting ground for diseases as Africans and Europeans freely exchanged infections to the detriment of Native Americans. Diseases of African origin included hookworm, dengue, and possibly yellow fever. Europeans brought smallpox, typhus, mumps (serious quinsy), whooping cough, and diphtheria. Native Americans probably suffered most from the interplay of diseases because they lacked the necessary immunities to protect themselves. The Cherokee and the remnants of the Catawba tribe in North Carolina were devastated by a smallpox epidemic in 1759 and 1760. Whites also suffered from epidemic diseases. Smallpox was reported in Halifax County in 1758, and the Moravians recorded typhus and whooping cough among members of their settlements in 1759 and 1769, respectively.

Europeans who immigrated to North Carolina often underwent a "seasoning process" by which they contracted malaria. Those who settled in the low, swampy areas of the eastern portions of the colony suffered most. Malaria, or the ague and fever, was particularly acute in autumn. On one occasion as many as nine people were buried in one day in Edenton alone. The "sickly season" was not always confined to the coastal region. The Moravians also suffered each fall and spring from similar illnesses which only cold weather could terminate.

Some residents of the colony, including Gov. William Tryon and Revolutionary patriot Cornelius Harnett, appreciated the therapeutic effects of the coastal air and water, and sent their families to the North Carolina seashore or to New England to recover their health.

Malaria, however, was more a debilitating disease than a killer. It weakened the system, reducing resistance to other diseases that in turn caused death. The consequences of malarial infection were manifold. By enervating its victims, malaria lowered the quantity and quality of labor. By hastening death from other diseases, malaria affected social and familial relationships. The resulting premature deaths, orphanage, and high rates of remarriage produced, in effect, a society of open and mixed households. Moreover, the prospect of short lives may have produced a proclivity toward a freer, more unrestrained life-style, particularly among males.

Mortality was greatest among infants and children. The experience of the Anglican congregation in St. Philip's Parish, Charleston, South Carolina, was probably representative of North Carolina. In 1756 in St. Philip's Parish, 35 of 105 recorded deaths were those of children under three years of age. Still, some colonials lived long lives. In 1772 six men in Carteret County petitioned for exemption from public taxes because of their advanced ages. One was sixty, three over sixty, one seventy, and one ninety. Then, of course, the elderly were afflicted with diseases peculiar to old age, such as heart conditions and nephritis, which was termed fits, dropsy, and decay.

In eighteenth-century England the medical profession consisted of physicians, surgeons, and apothecaries. Physicians were the elite of the medical profession. They usually held university degrees, practiced largely among the upper class, were "internists," and enjoyed the title "doctor" whatever their degree. Surgeons received training by apprenticeship and hospital work, worked chiefly on external problems, and were addressed as "mister." Apothecaries also lacked the elevated status of physicians; they sold and sometimes prescribed drugs.

In the colonies the above distinctions were blurred. Most of the doctors were surgeon apothecaries rather than the distinguished, scholarly gentlemen physicians. They merely assumed the title of doctor. There seemed to be no lack of surgeon apothecaries, or "doctors," in the more populous regions of the provinces. Throughout the colonies the ratio of doctors to population approximated 1 to 600, and in the urban areas, for example New York in 1750, the ratio dropped to 1 to 350. In Wilmington, North Carolina, at least twenty-four doctors practiced before 1778, which in any given year probably would have provided the town with a better ratio than the New York figure. Among the Wilmington practitioners were Armand John DeRosset and Moses John DeRosset, father and son. Three other Wilmington physicians were linked by Rebecca Green, daughter of Dr. Samuel Green, who first married Dr. John Mortimer and upon his death, Dr. James Geekie.

Dr. Abraham Blackall of Chowan County was a prominent physician in early North Carolina. Active in 1742, he treated a Mr. and Mrs. Ross, using pills, powders, gargles, lotions, purges, and bleeding for their various ailments. Later that year Dr. Blackall administered a purge, several doses of febrifuge powders, and a vial of Peruvian drops to Peter Trudeau to combat what was most probably malaria.

The Moravians provided Piedmont settlers with several well-trained physicians. Dr. Hans Martin Kalberlahn served Wachovia and the surrounding area from 1753 to 1759, when he died in a typhus epidemic. Patients came to Dr. Kalberlahn from as far away as one hundred miles. He successfully completed several operations, including trepanning (removing a piece of cranial bone) the head of a man who had been struck by an ax. A Dr. Schubert and Dr. Jacob Bonn succeeded Dr. Kalberlahn in the Piedmont.

North Carolinians enjoyed the services of a small number of university-trained or degree-holding physicians, and not all were above reproach. Dr. Robert Lenox of Edenton disgraced himself by using his professional visits and ministrations in an attempt to seduce the wife of John Campbell. Fined a large sum of money and stripped of his office as justice of the peace, Dr. Lenox spent several years regaining his creditability. His restoration to public esteem may well have resulted from the realization that his expertise was indispensable.

Doctors, like many other creditors in North Carolina, found payment for their services slow and small. As Alexander Pope said:

> God and the Doctor we alike adore,
> But only when in danger, not before;
> The danger over, both are alike requited,
> God is forgotten and the Doctor slighted.

In some areas of North Carolina, if a patient thought a practitioner's fee was too high, it was customary to submit the matter to another doctor or doctors who might approve the fee or reduce the charge according to the friendliness of their relationship with their colleague.

Those unable or unwilling to use the professional services of a physician relied upon their own knowledge of medicine, supplemented perhaps by such popular manuals as *Every Man his own Doctor: Or, The Poor Planter's Physician*, first published in 1734. In that guide the author provided remedies for ailments that included ague, consumption, gout, sore throat, and yaws. His prescriptions consisted mostly of local "medicines," such as bear oil, deer dung, garlic, honey, mint, mustard, and sage.

Yaws may have been the tropical disease brought by Africans to the colonies but more probably referred to endemic (nonvenereal) syphilis, a product of primitive living conditions and rudimentary knowledge of sanitation and hygiene. In their late stages, yaws and endemic syphilis disfigured the face and palate, often leaving the victim without a nose. William Byrd observed several such persons as he surveyed the dividing line between Virginia and North Carolina in 1728. Actually, yaws was confined mostly to the Albemarle section of North Carolina and waned as health and hygiene improved.

The author of *Every Man his own Doctor* admitted that yaws or country distemper was "very hard to cure perfectly." Yet he prescribed a potent concoction made of sumac root and the barks of pine and Spanish oak, a gargle for the throat, and pills consisting of turpentine and deer dung to treat the disease. To avoid yaws he counseled his readers to eat little fresh pork, avoid swampy areas, and for men, not to "venture upon strange Wom[e]n." Altogether the advice probably served as well as any for a relatively poor and ignorant populace, living where physicians were few and where, as late as 1811, "quacks [were] abundant, & . . . privileged to boast."

*Education*

Education in terms of institutionalized instruction was closely allied with the Church of England, or Anglican Church. The first known schoolteacher in the colony was Charles Griffin, a lay reader of the Anglican Church who came from the West Indies in 1705 to open a school in Pasquotank County near Nixonton. Griffin departed the colony in 1709, ultimately to teach at the College of William and Mary, and was succeeded by the Reverend James Adams. By 1712 a Mr. Mashburn had opened another church-related school in Chowan County near Sarem on the Virginia border. Mashburn's school was so highly regarded that families many miles distant sent their children for instruction.

As settlement expanded, so did the number of schools. Anglican missionary James Moir taught in Brunswick in 1745, and the Reverend Alexander Stewart established a school in Hyde County in 1763. The Reverend Daniel Earl, rector of St. Paul's Parish in Chowan, opened a school at his home on the Chowan River about fifteen miles from Edenton in the 1750s. Assisted by his daughter Nancy, Earl not only offered his students formal disciplinary study but also instructed the people of the area in the cultivation of flax, methods of weaving, and even the art of shad and herring fishing, which earned him the nickname of the "Herring-catching Parson."

The Moravians gave careful attention to the education of their children, though the first settlements did not include enough young people to justify formal educational institutions. In 1762 separate schools were established in Bethabara for the boys and girls of the town. About the same time, a school was opened in Bethania, which was three miles from Bethabara, and in 1771 the little community of Friedburg offered instruction to its youth. The next year a girls' school opened in Salem, followed in 1774 by a boys' school. Generally, the education provided by the Moravian schools did not continue beyond the fundamentals of reading, writing, and arithmetic, though a few boys and girls pursued their studies to enter academies in Pennsylvania.

Many nonsectarian public and private schools offered educational opportunities to the youth of North Carolina. The schools might be sponsored by a wealthy individual, initiated by an organized effort on the part of neighboring families, or instigated by an aspiring teacher. At least two individuals provided endowments in their wills for free schools. By his will in 1744, James Winwright of Carteret County appropriated all the rents and profits from his lands and houses in Beaufort for the hiring of a schoolmaster to teach reading, writing, and arithmetic to children of the area. Money was also set aside for the construction of a school and a house for the master. The results of the Winwright gift are not known, but within five years of its donation there was a schoolhouse at the Straits, not far from Beaufort. Col. James Innes of New Hanover County, by his will in 1760, also set aside money for a free school for "the benefit of the youth of North Carolina," but his legacy was not utilized until after the Revolution.

When free or private schools were unavailable, children received instruction from parents, older brothers and sisters, tutors, and itinerant schoolmasters. North Carolinians were concerned about the education of their children, and many stipulated in their wills that their children, grandchildren, nieces, and nephews should be educated in the best manner possible. Mary Conway wanted her son schooled in such a fashion as to qualify him "for such business or profession as his Genius shall most incline to." Edward Moseley recommended that one of his sons be trained in the law, "it being highly necessary in so Large a Family."

The children of the poor and orphans were not neglected. In addition to the free schools envisioned by Winwright, Innes, and possibly others, numerous legacies were left to the poor. John Bennett of Currituck County bequeathed forty shillings to educate two poor children for one year. Orphans with sufficient estates were placed with guardians who would educate and provide for the children "according to their Rank & degree." Otherwise the orphans were apprenticed to learn a handicraft or trade and at the same time to read and write.

An examination of orphans' accounts in Edgecombe from 1757 to 1774 finds general compliance with the legal mandates to educate the children. Among wards, nine of seventeen girls for whom more than two years of accounts exist received some education. Similar accounts for the boys show that twenty-six of thirty-six acquired schooling. Of course, these figures understate the total number of children exposed to formal instruction because some accounts are incomplete and others begin after some children had obtained their education. Moreover, the omission from the record of expenditures for schooling, as was the case for William Davis, is deceiving since the purchase of textbooks and paper for the young man, which is included, obviously denotes exposure to a formal learning process.

Although the laws of the province merely directed masters and mistresses of apprenticed orphans to teach the children to read and write, the county courts often took the spirit of the statutes more seriously. Edgecombe justices ordered James Ricks to give his apprentice at least one year of schooling as soon as possible. The Rowan court frequently demanded that masters provide apprentices with eighteen months of education, during which the children were to learn to read, write legibly, and "cypher to the five common rules." Moreover, the Rowan justices required that the children be raised "in the Protestant Christian Religion."

Efforts to educate African Americans derived principally from Dr. Bray's Associates, an English philanthropic organization that worked through the Anglican Church to bring religious instruction to young blacks. The Associates apparently considered erecting schools in the Cape Fear, Albemarle, and Bath areas in North Carolina. The efforts in the Cape Fear and Albemarle were futile, given the problems posed by transportation, the expense of boarding the children, the loss to masters of slave labor while the children were in school, and the "deeply rooted" prejudices of whites who objected to "their Children Associating with Slaves" and preferred that their slaves "remain Ignorant as brutes." As a result the Reverend Daniel Earl in Chowan County simply asked the Associates to assist in the education of white children.

Still, Anglicans realized some success in trying to extend the basics of education to slaves. With the Associates' aid the Reverend Alexander Stewart in the 1760s opened a school in Hyde County in which the schoolmistress and schoolmaster taught a small number of African American and Native American children. The Reverend John Barnett in Northampton County established two schools for adult slaves whose owners permitted their instruction in the evenings and on Sundays. An advertisement in a New Bern newspaper in 1752 for a runaway slave noted that the bondsman could "read, write, and cypher," an indication that educational opportunities were available for blacks, if not through the church, then perhaps from individual slaveholding families.

The quality of instruction offered to students varied greatly. Anglican ministers, such as the Reverend Thomas Burgess of Halifax County, usually possessed an extensive educational background. However, in Edgecombe County Thomas Bell augmented his

BY Permiſſion and Encouragement of the Truſtees the Public School Houſe of this Town is again opened, where Youth may be taught the Engliſh, Latin, or French Tongue; as alſo Writing, Arithmetic, Algebra, Trigonometry plain and ſpherical, Aſtronomy, Navigation, Surveying, Geography, the Uſe of the Globes, or any other Part of the Mathematics, the Italian Method of Bookkeeping, at the eſtabliſhed Price of the ſaid School, which may be known by enquiring of Mr. Davis, Printer of this Paper, and one of the Truſtees.

Newbern, Jun 30, 1775.

This notice for the reopening of a school in New Bern gives an indication of the variety of subjects taught in colonial schools. The advertisement appeared in the *North Carolina Gazette* (New Bern) on July 7, 1775.

carpenter's income with a teaching supplement, while Henry Tanton resorted to the classroom when old age and infirmities prevented him from active physical work. Janet Schaw stated that in the Wilmington area one of John Rutherfurd's sons hated his schoolmaster because the teacher knew so much less than the student.

The early schools in the colonial era were vague imitations of the Latin grammar schools in England. They provided a narrow curriculum that emphasized the classics and was designed to prepare students for college. Late in the colonial period, academies, distributors of education to the majority who would not go to college, became popular. Moreover, schoolmasters also indicated an increasing concern for a practical education, which became characteristic of the American educational process. Elias Hoell in 1774 offered Craven County residents two courses of study: reading, writing, ciphering, navigation, and surveying; and algebra, Euclid's *Elements*, Latin, and Greek. The next year Florence McCarthy, teacher of mathematics and the English language, opened an academy in New Bern where he taught English grammar, writing, arithmetic, Italian bookkeeping, navigation, gauging, algebra, geometry, trigonometry, surveying, and other subjects.

After the mid-eighteenth century, academies, forerunners of high schools, appeared in North Carolina. The most notable institution of education affiliated with the Anglican Church was the academy established in New Bern in 1764. The Reverend James Reed initiated the school in conjunction with a number of public-spirited citizens of New Bern and Craven County. Although the academy was supported primarily by a tax on imported liquors and legislative appropriations, the school was intended by its founders as a church school, remaining under the control of the church and exercising a religious influence on its pupils.

Thomas Tomlinson, who had emigrated from England at the instance of his brother who lived near New Bern, taught at the New Bern academy. From 1764 until his departure for Rhode Island in 1772, Tomlinson proved a capable teacher. He was faced with disciplinary problems, however, particularly because American parents often indulged their children. Tomlinson eventually incurred the enmity of two of the trustees of the school when he disciplined and expelled their children. Thereafter, one of the trustees sought to undermine the institution by curtailing its enrollment and stopping payment of Tomlinson's salary. Eventually Tomlinson was dismissed.

Another Anglican academy was established in Edenton. The legislature had authorized a school in the town in 1745, but the academy did not materialize until the 1760s, when citizens of Edenton erected a schoolhouse through a voluntary cooperative effort. Legislation in 1770 confirmed the institution and provided monetary support for it. Charles Pettigrew, a Presbyterian who became an Anglican minister, was appointed schoolmaster in 1773.

The immigration of Scotch-Irish and Germans stimulated education in the colony. The Reverend James Tate, a Presbyterian, opened perhaps the first classical academy in colonial North Carolina in Wilmington after moving to the town from Ireland in 1760. The most famous academy in the province was that of the Reverend David Caldwell, a graduate of Princeton College and a Presbyterian minister. Caldwell started his "Log College" in 1767 near Greensboro and enrolled fifty to sixty students each year. For forty years he trained future physicians, ministers, lawyers, judges, governors, and congressmen.

Higher education had to be obtained outside the colony. The wealthy sent their children to Virginia, Pennsylvania, New Jersey, New

England, and occasionally to Scotland and England to finish their schooling. Edward Moseley made provision for the education of his children after they had exhausted the resources of the "Common Masters" in North Carolina. Cullen Pollock instructed that his sons, after learning as much as possible in North Carolina, be sent to Boston for further education and remain there in the care of some prudent person until they reached the age of eighteen. John Pfifer of Mecklenburg County left funds for the education of his children, particularly his son Paul who was to "be put through a liberal Education and Colleged."

The college made a tardy appearance in North Carolina. The first effort to establish a college was made in 1754 when the legislature provided funds for an institution to "promote good order, Literature, and true Religion, in all parts of this province." Unfortunately, the French and Indian War, which began at that time, proved so costly that the college moneys were used for military purposes.

The idea of establishing a college was revived by Presbyterian residents of Mecklenburg County who persuaded Gov. William Tryon to recommend to the assembly the erection of a seminary in the backcountry. The assembly agreed and passed legislation in 1771 entitled "An Act for establishing and endowing of Queen's College in the Town of Charlotte in Mecklenburg County." The legislation pointed out the need for "a Seminary of Learning" for students who had obtained sufficient knowledge of Latin, Greek, and Hebrew and who could acquire the principles of "Science and Virtue" that would make them better citizens of their communities. Public tax moneys, private donations, and a lottery would support the institution.

The law stated that the president of the college must belong to the Anglican Church, but it did not specify that the "three or less tutors" had to be licensed by either the bishop of London or by the governor. That omission prompted the Crown to disallow the law in 1772. North Carolinians did not learn of that action until 1773, and by that time the college had already opened. Thereafter it continued to operate under the name of Queen's Museum without the benefit of legislative approval or public tax support. In 1777 it was rechartered under the name Liberty Hall Academy.

The new state constitution of 1776 envisioned the founding of one or more state-supported universities. Between 1776 and 1789 a large number of academies that served as high schools were chartered by the assembly in an attempt to prepare students for college study. Liberty Hall in Charlotte was one of those academies. After the turmoil of the Revolutionary years had abated, North Carolina became one of the first states to propose the establishment of a state-funded university and the first to open such an institution.

Despite the interest in colleges shown during the colonial era, few North Carolinians attended institutions of higher education. Three went to Harvard and one to the College of Philadelphia. None matriculated in the College of William and Mary in neighboring Virginia before 1771. Overseas three young men from the colony went to Eton, but none enrolled in Oxford or Cambridge between 1720 and 1776. Only 8 North Carolinians received instruction at the famed Inns of Court, as opposed to 58 from South Carolina, 43 from Virginia, 33 from Maryland, and 11 from Georgia.

Education, of course, encompassed more than academic instruction. Wyriot Ormond in 1773 warned his executors that no expense was too great for the education of his two daughters and added, "I not only mean that part of their Education which Respects their Schooling, but Every Other that Can be had for their Advantage." Gov. Gabriel Johnston elaborated on this point in his will in 1751:

I Earnestly Request my Dearest Wife be a kind tender Mother to my Dear little Girl, and to bring her up in the Fear of God and under a deep Sense of her being always in his Presence, and in Sobriety and Moderation Confining her Desires to things Plain, neat and Elegant, and not aspiring after the Gayety, Splendor and Extravagances; and Especially, to take Care to keep within the Bounds of her Incomes, and by no Means to Run in Debt.

The extent and nature of the book collections owned by Carolinians reflected their educational attainments as well as cultural concerns. Records indicate that at least two-thirds of the colonials owned books. Many possessed only a Bible. Most had five or more books, and some amassed large private libraries. The Reverend James Reed owned 266 volumes; Dr. John Eustace, 282; Edward Moseley, 400; James Milner, 621; and Samuel Johnston, over 1,000 in a collection started by his uncle, Governor Johnston. Most of Johnston's books dealt with topics in theology, moral philosophy, literature, history, law, and medicine. They were often written in Latin, Greek, Hebrew, and French, as well as in English.

*Welfare*

Poverty and the consequent need for welfare support came to characterize a small segment of the North Carolina population. Dr. John Brickell wrote from the Albemarle region about 1730 that "poverty is an entire stranger here." Although he was not altogether correct, at least the impoverished lived in the "Best poor mans Country I Ever heard of," according to one man in North Carolina in 1770. The colonials, however, utilized a broad definition of the poor, including not only the indigent but also the aged, widowed, orphaned, insane, sick, and disabled—in essence, those unable to help themselves.

Although families and friends undertook poor relief when possible, the burden often fell upon the public. The Anglican Church assumed primary responsibility for the poor, with respective parishes using tax moneys to alleviate the poverty and misery within their bounds. Available records indicate that St. Paul's Parish in Chowan County aided 134 individuals between 1712 and 1775; St. John's Parish in Carteret County, 41 between 1742 and 1775. Men constituted about 40 percent of the needy; women, 30 percent; children, 20 percent; and women with children, 10 percent.

The parishes preferred to allow the poor to live at home whenever possible. Psychologically, it benefited the indigent; financially, it benefited the parish. In 1775 St. Paul's Parish gave Elizabeth Thompson 1½ yards of cotton cloth, 5½ bushels of meal, 50 pounds of flour, and 2 gallons of molasses. The parish also paid for putting her under a "course of physic." In the same year the parish offered William Tibison and his sister Sarah 2 bushels of meal and 95 pounds of pork. In addition, William was the beneficiary of 3½ yards of cloth and Sarah of 30 pounds of bread and 10 pounds of flour.

When poverty mandated care outside the home, the poor were supported in community households rather than in public institutions, such as almshouses or workhouses. The responsibility for boarding the poor was diffused among many families in order to spread the burden. Most of the poor found a stable atmosphere in which to reside, but some were shunted from one home to another. At least eleven people kept Moses Welwood between 1765 and 1772, and sixteen people boarded Rachel Purvine from 1741 to her death in 1753.

Although few of the poor remained on relief for more than four years, the aid dispensed by vestries in those instances revealed the extensive care bestowed on them. St. Paul's first assisted Rachel Purvine in 1740 after Richard Bond, churchwarden, expended forty shillings on his own initiative to help that "poor woman in great want of assistance from the parish." In 1744 the vestry ordered that Purvine be taken to Cosander Springs, presumably a spa, and by 1747 had purchased shifts, gowns, caps of fine linen, and shoes for her. Few of the parish accounts are as detailed as that for Robert Alphin, who was placed on relief in St. John's in 1755. At that time the parish paid Elizabeth Hinton for curing his hand. Later that year it purchased $2\frac{3}{4}$ yards of bearskin, $3\frac{1}{2}$ yards of checks, 8 yards of osnaburg, 2 stick twists, 2 dozen buttons, a linen handkerchief, and a pair of shoes for Alphin. Just before Alphin's death the parish recorded expenditures for 7 yards of osnaburg, $2\frac{1}{2}$ yards of cloth, a dozen buttons, a pair of stockings, and a worsted cap.

Occasionally a parish attempted to centralize care for the poor by contracting with an individual to take charge of all the indigent within the parish. In May 1742 the churchwardens of St. Paul's were ordered to bring all the poor of the parish to the next vestry meeting. Any person who was willing to board the poor was asked to appear at the meeting to arrange financial terms for the service. Thomas Walton kept the poor for six months; Orlando Champion housed most of them for the following six months. Nathaniel Hocutt succeeded Champion but served only a short time. The needy were then again separated and placed in different households. The only other indication that an individual had contracted to care for the indigent was a payment by St. Paul's in 1774 to Nathaniel Jones for maintaining several of the parish poor. Selected individuals also provided certain services for the poor. For a time the vestry of St. Paul's turned to Thomas Walton to procure shoes for all the needy, and in 1772 and 1773 Dr. Samuel Dickinson provided medical care for the poor in St. Paul's Parish. Otherwise, aid was usually rendered by the parish on an individual, selective basis.

The supervision of orphans constituted the principal contribution of the county governments to poor relief. Orphans, as minors, represented an element of the poor who depended upon the public for protection, support, and care until they attained their legal majority. Those with sufficient estates were placed with guardians who educated and provided for the children "according to their Rank & degree." The less fortunate, including illegitimate children, were apprenticed to learn a handicraft or trade.

Not only did the county courts appoint guardians and apprentice children, they also attempted to protect the young ones. Guardians gave bonded security to protect the estates of their wards. The guardians submitted annual reports of their wards' financial affairs to the courts. The courts also sought to protect apprentices from abusive masters and to make sure that the children were taught a handicraft and the rudiments of education.

The counties also expended money directly to assist the poor, though the courts preferred that the parishes undertake such expenses. Most county money went to the sick. Between 1758 and 1774 Chowan, Craven, and New Hanover Counties provided funds for those stricken with smallpox. Craven also bought supplies for vessels riding quarantine off New Bern, and Rowan, with a relatively weak Anglican establishment, often proffered small sums to the sick and needy in St. Luke's Parish.

The provincial government eased the burden of the poor by permitting them to secure exemptions from taxes and public services (working on the roads and attending musters). An exemption was obtained by petitioning the county court, which ordered the clerk to prepare a certificate to the General Assembly. A legislative representative from the county presented the petition to the assembly. Applicants were rarely denied. The counties approved 99 percent of them, and the assembly gave almost perfunctory approval.

The justifications for exemptions provide insight into the nature of poverty in the colony. Age and mental or physical disability were the predominant factors. Once a man reached sixty, and poverty, probably caused by infirmity, attended his condition, he could seek exemption. John Hicks of Chowan claimed that he was "advanced to the age of Sixty Six Years, very infirm & Poor[,] and unable to labour." New Hanover accepted Thomas Skinner's petition, "he appearing to be upwards of Sixty Years of Age." Onslow justices received favorably the petitions of John Berkenpine and Jacob Biddle, who were "Very Ancient."

The other principal category of exemptions consisted of the mentally and physically disabled. Ephraim Chadwick of Carteret told the court that his son "was in a Deplorable Condition by the Loss of his Reason and by severall other Infirmaties," and John Granade reported that his son was "a person very Lame and Infirm and much Troubled with Fits." Mental illness appeared to be relatively rare, however, and cases of exemptions involving physical conditions were far more numerous than those for mental disorders. Hugh Rigby of Craven petitioned "on Account of the loss of his Eye Sight and infirmities and Poverty." A heartrending summation of physical disability can be seen in the six petitions to the Rowan County court in 1766: William and James Story were "Unable to help them Selves by having No Use of their Limbs"; Henry Evans and Alexander Hughes were deaf and dumb; John Loss had lost the sight in one eye and had only partial vision in the other; and Fredrick Goss, "Extreamly helpless," was utterly unable to do the least work.

For those who were imprisoned because they were unable to pay their creditors, the colony provided a remedy through legislation for the relief of "poor debtors." Statutes in 1749 and 1762 permitted debtors to be absolved from their obligations and to obtain their freedom if they possessed an estate worth less than forty shillings, exclusive of wearing apparel, working tools, and arms for militia musters. Those sued for debt who were worth more than forty shillings also had the opportunity to escape incarceration by delivering their estates in trust to their creditors.

An examination of the extant court minutes of eleven counties before the Revolution produced only fifty-four petitions from persons seeking relief because of insolvency. Two were denied, one was appealed to superior court, and the rest were favorably received. Two of the successful petitioners were women, Esther Robinson of Orange County and Elizabeth Guy of New Hanover County. Richard Cannon was also among the petitioners. His meager estate, which only slightly exceeded the forty shilling limit, consisted of an "old" flock bed, a blanket, an "old" basin, four plates, an "old" spinning wheel, seven pounds of wool, a punch bowl, two flag mats, an "old" frying pan, two knives, two forks, and an "old" pail.

The colony also aided the poor by awarding grants or pensions to men who suffered disabilities in military service and to families of men who died in the service of the colony. Robert Campbell, who served in the French and Indian War, was wounded and scalped. Disabled by the injuries, he desired to go to Europe to live with relatives, and the province granted him fifty pounds for that purpose. After the Battle of Alamance in 1771, when Gov. William Tryon and eastern militia defeated the Regulators, widows of deceased soldiers sought relief. Faithy Smith, "a very poor and distressed Widow with an Infant at her Breast," was granted support by the legislature.

The poor were not neglected in colonial North Carolina. Although the province lacked an extended and sophisticated system of poor relief, a variety of indigents benefited directly or indirectly from public support. The colony recognized a community responsibility for the less fortunate and acted upon that obligation within the confines of limited experience and restricted funds.

CHAPTER SIX

# RELIGION

The state of religion in colonial North Carolina remained unstable from the first settlements to the outbreak of the Revolution. The isolation of the colony, the change in ownership from the proprietors to the Crown, and the continual immigration of disparate peoples contributed to the unsettled situation. Gov. William Tryon wrote in 1765 that every religious denomination except Catholicism abounded in the colony. The diversity of denominations, however, did not ensure a religious populace. Anglican minister Charles Woodmason observed in the mid-1760s that "As to North Carolina, the State of Religion therein, is greatly to be lamented—If it can be said, That there is any Religion, or a Religious Person in it." As a partisan member of the Anglican Church, which was confronted with fierce sectarian competition, Woodmason, of course, exaggerated. Still, his assessment of the religious climate in North Carolina contained an element of truth.

Upon the founding of Carolina the Lords Proprietors had sanctioned religious toleration in order to entice immigrants to their colony, but at the same time they had given official encouragement to the Anglican Church, or Church of England. For thirty years the Anglicans remained unwilling or unable to take advantage of their privileged position. Not a single Anglican minister entered the province before 1700, and a well-organized Quaker faction dominated the religious scene.

St. Thomas Church in Bath is the oldest existing church in North Carolina. Construction on this simple rectangular structure began in 1734. Photograph from the files of the Division of Archives and History.

By the turn of the eighteenth century, the appointment of zealous Anglican governors and the appearance of Anglican missionaries from England upset the religious calm of the province. Legislation in 1701 and 1703 provided for the establishment of the Anglican Church in the colony. Nevertheless, the superior status of the Church of England was not secured for another eight years. Quaker opposition to the establishment and the "rebellion" of former governor Thomas Cary in 1708-1711 delayed the implementation of the Anglican establishment. But in 1711 newly appointed governor Edward Hyde, reportedly a distant cousin of Queen Anne, successfully repulsed Cary's armed resistance to the government and definitely confirmed the Anglican position.

The establishment apparently failed to benefit the Anglicans. The church never evinced widespread strength or appeal in North Carolina. The proprietors continually slighted the province in favor of South Carolina, while after 1729, when the Crown purchased North Carolina, the close association between the Crown and the church often aroused hostile feelings. Non-Anglicans resented paying taxes for the support of the church, opposed the church's control over education, and decried other special privileges, including the exclusive right of Anglican ministers to solemnize marriages. The ritual of the church, the failure to emphasize preaching, and aristocratic bias connoted a lack of emotional appeal that seriously curtailed the popularity of Anglicanism.

The absence of a resident bishop also retarded the growth of the Anglican Church. North Carolina governors continually importuned London for a bishop to ordain prospective ministers, restrain clergymen who acted immoderately, and remove those guilty of malfeasance. The bishop of London and the Crown spurned the requests. The consequence of this decision was twofold: a long and dangerous journey to England for ordination, during which some prospective ministers perished, and a lack of restraint upon the clergy resident in America.

Of the fewer than fifty Anglican clergymen sent to North Carolina before 1775, the Society for the Propagation of the Gospel in Foreign Parts (SPG), founded in 1701 by the Reverend Thomas Bray and associates, dispatched thirty-three. The SPG intended to send Anglican missionaries throughout the British empire for the purpose of offering divine worship and education to all English subjects, including blacks and Native Americans. The society, however, slighted North Carolina, partly because the Carolinians seldom received missionaries very cordially and partly because physical dangers threatened those who challenged the Carolina wilderness. The Reverend John Rainsford slept in an old tobacco barn, and the Reverend John Urmstone was forced to subsist for some time on a dry crust of bread and salt water. The Reverend Ebenezer Taylor died as a result of remaining adrift in the Albemarle Sound for ten days in bitterly cold weather. The missionaries recognized the uninviting situation of the colony. In fact, the Reverend John Blair called the province "the most barbarous place in the Continent" in 1704 and immediately departed from the area.

Despite the adverse geographic and climatic conditions, many able and conscientious ministers served the Anglican Church in North Carolina. The Reverend Clement Hall, who officiated in St. Paul's Parish, Edenton, and the four northeastern counties in the colony from 1744 until his death in 1759, typified that group. In addition to preaching regularly in St. Paul's Parish, Hall usually journeyed through his mission territory at least twice a year. Seldom were his trips less than 200 miles, and on one occasion he traveled 557 miles in a thirty-six-day period. In 1755 Hall estimated that he traveled 2,200 miles a year. He also went to Granville County and several times preached in Virginia in his efforts to reach those who desired the benefits of religious services. Hall's careful accounts of his labors indicate that he preached to congregations of as many as six hundred people, administered Holy Communion to three hundred people on a single tour, and baptized at least ten thousand people during his ministry.

While many of the clergymen were devoted, zealous, selfless individuals, there were others who were acknowledged scoundrels and whose activities besmirched the reputation of the entire ministry. Daniel Brett, the first Anglican minister in the colony, "brought great grief and shame to the friends of the Church" by his actions. The Reverend Michael Smith served the parishes in Johnston and New Hanover Counties from 1758 to 1760 but was dismissed by the SPG when his sordid past in South Carolina was revealed. In the southern colony he had lived with a woman without the benefit of marriage vows, retired to a tavern on Sundays after preaching, played billiards immediately after giving the Holy Sacrament, and defrauded his parish of considerable money. The Reverend John Boyd of the Brunswick region in North Carolina was seen on a Sunday in the spring of 1737 "at noon day, . . . Lying dead Drunk & fast asleep on the Great Road to Virginia, with his Horse Bridle tyed to his Leg." About two years later it was reported that Boyd was dead and that he had died "in the same Beastly way he lived."

The quality of the Anglican ministry is understandable. North Carolina had little to offer the more able ministers. Salaries were always low and inflation continually reduced the value of such stipends. Although the vestries supposedly taxed the inhabitants to pay the ministers, the vestries often failed to levy the tax, or the sheriffs who collected the moneys used the funds for their own purposes. The fact that most of the Anglican ministers were sent by the SPG and partially maintained by the society indicates the lack of support rendered by the colonials. Furthermore, there were no outstanding parish churches to which ambitious young clergymen could be appointed. In most of the parishes in the colony, the majority of those claiming religious affiliation embraced some denomination other than

St. Paul's Church served the Anglican parishioners of Edenton. Construction began in 1736 and was completed in 1774. The spire was added in 1809. Photograph from the files of the Division of Archives and History.

Anglicanism. Thus the Anglican ministers rarely received moral or monetary support from their parishes. Governor Tryon, a zealous Anglican, lamented that there were no gradations of church preferments. The situation was deplorable, according to Tryon, because "human industry is generally excited by future prospects of reward in this world, as well as by their hopes of greater in the next." Hence men of small ability, no influence, and often little religion accepted assignments in North Carolina, and those reluctantly.

Anglican parishes, as basic units of polity in the colonies and mother country, combined civil as well as ecclesiastical functions. Since the parishes antedated the counties in the early settlement of Virginia, they sometimes assumed civil responsibilities that did not fall within the purview of their counterparts in England. In the case of North Carolina, first settled by Virginians and naturally inclined to emulate the northern colony, example and necessity joined to promote such parochial civil duties as caring for the poor and providing weights and measures. However, the increasing competency of the civil authority in the form of the county court resulted in stripping the parishes of most of their nonecclesiastical functions by the time of the Revolution.

Legislation in 1702 directed each parish in North Carolina to obtain a set of weights and measures to serve as a standard for public use. Ordered from Boston, the weights and measures for St. Paul's Parish— a brass yard, a pair of brass scales, a one-gallon pewter wine pot, a half bushel, a peck, and a quarter pot—arrived the following year and were lodged eventually with vestryman Nicholas Crisp. Subsequently Crisp or the parish misplaced the items. Legislation in 1741 transferred responsibility for the standard to the county courts. Although no reason was given for the change, the seeming inability of the parishes to maintain the standards and the maturity of the county courts as governmental units may have contributed to the decision.

Parishes briefly assumed the responsibility for payments for the destruction of vermin or annoying and destructive animals (wolves, panthers, wildcats, squirrels). Although the county courts and then the colonial treasurer first underwrote that expense, legislation in 1738 placed that burden upon the parishes. In May 1740 St. Paul's vestry directed the churchwardens to "pay Each and Every person which produces a certificate for a Lawfull Claim Relating to the Vermine act. . . ." A statute in 1748 reiterated the strictures of the earlier legislation, but in 1757 the assembly determined that the 1748 law did not "answer the good purposes intended thereby" and repealed the act. Later enactments made the county courts accountable for vermin payments.

The growth and spread of dissenting sects—Quakers, Lutherans, German Reformed, Dunkers (Church of the Brethren), Moravians, Presbyterians, Baptists, and Methodists—constituted a significant development in North Carolina religious life during the royal era. The Quakers represented the earliest element of organized religion in the province. William Edmundson, a missionary, helped to introduce Quakerism to the colony in 1672. When George Fox, founder of Quakerism in England, later arrived in the Albemarle area, he found a small but thriving nucleus of Friends. Since there was no other formal religion, church, or ministry in North Carolina at the time, Fox had ample opportunity to make more converts. Still, he and fellow missionaries had to endure severe hardships. Roads were practically nonexistent, while fording the many creeks and rivers was hazardous. Edmundson, on a second visit to the province in 1676-1677, braved Indian hostilities along the Virginia border in order to enter North Carolina.

The incidence of Quaker conversions increased rapidly and resulted in organized meetings at the regional and provincial levels. Monthly meetings were held at the house of Francis Toms at least as early as 1680. An Eastern Quarterly Meeting was established about 1681 for Friends in Pasquotank, Perquimans, and present-day Northampton Counties. The first North Carolina Yearly Meeting was instituted in 1698.

Although the number of Quakers in North Carolina is impossible to determine exactly, several Anglican missionaries estimated their adherents at one-seventh to one-tenth of the total population. Those Anglicans characterized the Quakers as extremely ignorant, insufferably proud, and ungovernable. It is possible, however, to discern a certain tacit admiration for the Quakers by the Anglican ministers, who appreciated their godliness and the ease with which they made converts. And the Anglican clergy were forced to admit that many embraced Quakerism in reaction to the poor example set by the Anglicans, preferring any religion to none at all.

Between 1725 and 1775 a large migration of Quakers from Pennsylvania and more northerly areas contributed to an increase of Friends in North Carolina as well as a broadening of the Quaker geographical base in the colony. Early Quakerism was confined principally to the Albemarle region, though Quakers were scattered throughout the eastern counties. The new immigrants settled in Alamance, Chatham, Guilford, Randolph, and Surry Counties. One of the most influential of these settlements was New Garden in Guilford County, which was established about 1750. A monthly meeting by that name was held in 1754. Most of the later Quaker meetings in the area emanated from the New Garden community. In 1771 an even larger migration of Quakers from Nantucket, Rhode Island, substantially increased the number of Friends in the middle portions of North Carolina. The influence of the Quakers continued to grow until the outbreak of the Revolution when hostilities curtailed the activities of the pacifist Friends.

German religious adherents, most prominent in the Piedmont, represented four sects primarily: Lutheran, Reformed, Dunker, and Moravian. The Lutherans, probably the most numerous of the German sects, settled in Rowan, Cabarrus, Stanly, Davidson, and other central Piedmont counties. The Reformed adherents gravitated to the same communities. Both groups were without ministers upon their arrival in the colony in the late 1740s. The Reverend Christian Theus, a Reformed minister from South Carolina, preached in North Carolina in the 1750s and 1760s, and Samuel Suther later officiated at Grace Church in Rowan and the two other Reformed churches in Davidson. The Lutherans in the meantime had organized three churches—Zion and St. John's in Rowan and St. John's in Cabarrus County. In 1773 the Lutheran churches successfully secured a schoolmaster and a minister from Germany, Johann Gottfried Arndt and Adolph Nussman, respectively.

The Dunkers, whose name arose from the practice of total immersion, originated in Germany in 1708. Members of the sect attempted to imitate the Christians of the first century, which led them to adopt baptism by trine immersion, pacifism, rejection of courts to settle disputes, and great plainness in language and dress. The Dunkers established at least six settlements in North Carolina in the eighteenth century, but only two survived to become congregations

August Gottlieb Spangenberg, a German native, was bishop of the Moravian Church. In 1752-1753 he led a group to survey the land that would become the Moravian settlement in North Carolina. Spangenberg selected the name Wachovia. Portrait photograph from the files of the Division of Archives and History.

in the twentieth-century Church of the Brethren. The older is the Fraternity Church of the Brethren located six miles southwest of Winston-Salem; the other is the Flat Rock congregation of New River in Ashe County.

The Moravians were Protestants and followers of the Unitas Fratrum, mid-fifteenth century supporters of John Hus in Bohemia. The North Carolina Moravians were an offshoot of the Pennsylvania group. Bishop August Spangenberg led a party to survey prospective lands in North Carolina in 1752 for possible settlement. Subsequently 99,985 acres were purchased by the Moravians from Earl Granville in a tract that was called Wachovia. The first party of permanent Moravian settlers reached Wachovia in November 1753. They and their successors established a thriving, self-contained settlement where the Moravians could practice their social, religious, and economic customs.

The Moravians by their unusual life-style, which stressed communal and cooperative endeavors, aroused some suspicions. Through organized and cooperative effort the group succeeded in establishing a Christian community, aiding their neighbors, and spreading the gospel on the very edge of the frontier. The deep sense of religion within the Moravian settlement spoke for itself, but equally laudable was their attempt to minister to the needs of other Christians in the area who were without benefit of church or clergy. When English-speaking visitors were present in Wachovia, services would be held in English. Moravians also visited neighbors in their homes and held services for them. They freely administered baptismal rites to children but never claimed by such action that the children were members of the Moravian Church. Had the Moravians attempted to convert other North Carolinians, they might have been quite successful, but they were satisfied to bring the gospel to those in need and allow others to reap the fertile religious harvest which they sowed.

The Scotch-Irish introduced Presbyterianism to North Carolina as an organized church. William Robinson in 1742 was the first known Presbyterian minister to visit the colony, and he was followed by other itinerant preachers. The most famous of these missionaries was Hugh McAden, who left a detailed record of his endeavors. McAden first toured the colony in 1755 and 1756; he encountered at least seven Presbyterian houses of worship and many worshiping communities, but few organized churches and no resident ministers. McAden proceeded to visit some fifty communities where he usually preached in private homes or in open fields. He established at least seven churches between the Hyco and Yadkin Rivers.

McAden persuaded the Reverend James Campbell to settle in the colony in 1758 to minister to the needs of the numerous Highland Scots living along the Cape Fear River. Campbell customarily preached two sermons on Sundays—one in Gaelic for the Highlanders and one in English for the less numerous Lowlanders and Scotch-Irish in the area. Campbell trained his listeners well, for in 1770 the Reverend John McLeod said that he would rather preach to the most sophisticated congregation in Edinburgh than to "the little critical carls" along the Cape Fear.

In 1758 the Reverend Alexander Craighead settled permanently in North Carolina. After Gen. Edward Braddock's disastrous defeat, Indians had driven Craighead and his congregation from Virginia to North Carolina where they took refuge in Mecklenburg County. Craighead became pastor of the Rocky River and Sugar Creek churches and was the only Presbyterian minister between the Yadkin and Catawba Rivers during the early 1760s.

McAden returned to the colony in 1759 to become the pastor of congregations in Duplin and New Hanover Counties. Joining McAden, Campbell, and Craighead in the colony were such distinguished ministers as David Caldwell, Samuel E. McCorkle, and the particularly influential Henry Pattillo. In 1770 Presbyterians in North and South Carolina were organized into the Orange Presbytery, which included twelve congregations in the two colonies. The Presbyterians in North Carolina organized at least forty-four churches in the province before 1780 and exercised an influence in the colony's politics, especially in the backcountry, far in excess of their proportionate numbers in the province.

Outstripping the Presbyterians and Quakers in popularity were the Baptists of one variety or another. While some individual Baptists may have been present in the colony in the seventeenth century, the first organized Baptist congregation appeared only in 1727, founded by the Reverend Paul Palmer near Cisco in Chowan County. The early congregations were General Baptists who offered salvation to all who repented and submitted to baptism. During the next two decades Baptist missionaries worked so effectively that by 1752 they claimed sixteen congregations and several hundred members. The Kehukee Baptist Association was formed in 1769 from churches in Halifax, Edgecombe, Martin, Washington, Beaufort, Carteret, other eastern counties, and a few South Carolina counties. By the outbreak of the Revolution, this group alone accounted for sixty-one churches and five thousand members.

In the 1750s the Separate Baptists challenged the older General Baptists. The Separates sprang from New England revivalism. The establishment of the Sandy Creek Church in 1755 in Guilford County by Shubal Stearns signaled the inauguration of the Separatist advent in North Carolina. These Baptists stressed the autonomy of each congregation and weekly communion, believed in nine Christian rites including the Lord's Supper and Baptism, and accepted "eldresses" and "deaconesses." Their religious gatherings, often in the camp-meeting style, frequently culminated in fits, frenzied jerking, talking in tongues, and other expressions of zeal that alarmed people of the more conservative denominations. Whereas the General Baptists had sought converts, they had not offended the Anglicans in the process. The Separates were not so reserved, and their appeal seemed irresistible. In 1758 the Sandy Creek Association, the oldest Baptist association in North Carolina, was formed, and within two decades at least forty-two Separate churches had been established in the colony. By 1775 the Baptists probably constituted the largest denomination in North Carolina and presented the most formidable opposition to the established Anglican Church.

The last major Protestant denomination to secure a foothold in North Carolina before the Revolution was Methodism. A product of John Wesley's religious experience and maturation, Methodism had been an organized movement in England thirty years before its missionaries were sent to America. Between 1769 and 1774 Wesley dispatched to the colonies eight such emissaries, of whom Francis Asbury remained to become the father of American Methodism.

Methodism was immediately popular in the Middle Atlantic and southern colonies, particularly in Virginia and North Carolina. Relatively democratic church organization, a degree of local autonomy, and evangelical fervor enhanced its appeal. The failure of the established church to minister to the spiritual needs of the people and the existence of a large number of churchless inhabitants contributed to the success of the Methodist movement.

The first Methodist minister to reach North Carolina was Joseph Pilmore who preached a sermon in the province in September 1772 at the Currituck County courthouse. Two years later North Carolina Methodists were sufficiently numerous to be included in the first Virginia circuit, which extended from Petersburg to the Albemarle counties. By 1776 North Carolina's 683 Methodists justified a circuit of their own. By that time northeastern North Carolina and southern Virginia had become the cradle of southern Methodism in one of the biggest revivals ever experienced by the Methodist Church in America.

Governor Tryon was correct when he implied that Roman Catholics were few in North Carolina. Their number and disparity prevented them from organizing worship services. The Reverend Thomas Newman, an Anglican missionary, stated in 1722 that there were no more than a dozen Catholics in the colony. The Reverend John Garzia reported nine in his parish of St. Thomas in 1741; the Reverend Clement Hall found none in St. Paul's Parish in the 1740s; the Reverend James Reed in 1760 believed that there were no more than nine or ten in Craven County. However, in 1752 counterfeiter Daniel Johnston, a "staunch Roman Catholick," was hanged in New Bern. Johnston, a Jacobite, went to his death hoping that the Scottish spirit of rebellion against the English Hanoverian usurpers was still alive.

Joseph Pilmore was a native of Yorkshire, England, and a Methodist missionary to the American colonies. In 1772-1773 during a journey from the northern colonies to Savannah, Georgia, he became the first Methodist minister to visit North Carolina. Portrait from the files of the Division of Archives and History.

Jews were even fewer in number than Catholics. Some may have resided in early Wilmington, but most assertions of Jews resident in colonial North Carolina are conjectural. However, one definite Jewish inhabitant of the province was "the wife of Christian Frey" in Bethabara, "a Jewess by birth," according to the *Moravian Records*.

Despite the establishment of the Anglican Church and the rapid strides made by the dissenting sects, North Carolinians remained a comparatively unchurched people, as the Methodists found in the 1770s. Contemporary Virginia historian Hugh Jones wrote in *The Present State of Virginia* that "Religion cannot be expected among a Collection of such People as fly thither from other Places for Safety and Livelihood, left to their own Liberty without Restraint or Instruction." Many had "but the bare name of God and Christ; and that too frequently in nothing but vain Swearing, Cursing, and Imprecations."

The North Carolina government attempted to remedy the lax moral situation by statute, but the difficulties of legislating morality were quickly perceived. At least as early as 1715, the provincial assembly enacted legislation to encourage the observance of Sunday as a holy day. The law directed everyone to engage in some form of private or public worship on Sunday and forbade any labor, including hunting and fishing, on the Sabbath. Slaves were similarly restricted in their activities.

The legislators also noted that "the odious & loathsome Sin of Drunkenness" had become a common occurrence in the colony. Since this was the foundation of many iniquitous practices, the law contained a provision for levying fines on those who became intoxicated on the Sabbath. Furthermore, tavern keepers were forbidden to sell any alcoholic beverages on Sundays except to travelers. Later this restriction was relaxed to permit the sale of liquors on Sundays before and after church hours, but tavern keepers were warned not to allow anyone to become drunk.

The legislation of 1715 contained further admonitions against other prevalent immoral activities. Profane cursing, mentioned by Jones, and common-law marriages were prohibited. A similar statute in 1741 reiterated many of the provisions of the earlier law and pointedly observed that clergymen in the colony were not exempt from the penalties of the law.

Despite the laws many North Carolinians remained ignorant of religion. This seemed particularly true in the backcountry where the inhabitants were somewhat isolated and civilization was in its elementary stages. The people of western North Carolina were occupied by the rigors of building homes and extracting livelihoods from the wilderness. They often lived and behaved in the manner of the Indians with whom they vied for the land. Thus a polished, learned, and godly individual such as the Reverend Charles Woodmason might easily declare that the manners of North Carolinians were vile and corrupt, that the colony was a scene of debauchery and dissoluteness, and that the people lived in a state of polygamy, illegitimacy, and concubinage.

The situation in the east was only slightly better than that in the backcountry. Josiah Quincy Jr., the intercolonial traveler and journalist from Massachusetts, noted that many of the political and social leaders of the Cape Fear area ignored the laws relative to religion and the observance of the Sabbath. He concluded that it was time either to repeal such laws or to attempt better enforcement. The validity of his observations was supported by the need in Beaufort and Wilmington to have constables patrol the streets near places of worship during church hours to disperse noisy persons who disturbed worshipers. In

Wilmington, however, the constables were remiss in their duty, an indication of their less than faithful observance of the Sabbath.

This state of religion was hardly surprising. Religion throughout the southern colonies as well as in England appeared to have been lackluster in its appeal and influence in the mid-eighteenth century. In North Carolina the populace was very poor and unable to support adequately church construction and ministers of any denomination. Churches rotted, stood half-finished, or became shelters for hogs and cattle. Difficulties of travel and communication, particularly severe in North Carolina, hampered all social interaction, including religious gatherings. This condition was reinforced by the colony's lack of large urban centers, which would have congregated people and fostered cultural development as in New England.

Nevertheless, the more positive aspects of religious development in the colony should not be overlooked. The Anglican parishes performed valuable social as well as religious functions. In addition, the Anglican Church attempted to carry the elements of Christianity to blacks and Native Americans in the colony. Throughout the eighteenth century the first missionaries from the Society for the Propagation of the Gospel tried to convert blacks, but they were partially thwarted early in the century by the prevailing contention among planters that the baptism of a slave constituted his liberation. This belief slowly eroded during the proprietary era, and by the 1730s Anglican ministers began to baptize slaves. The Reverend Charles Cupples of Bute County wrote the SPG in 1768 that he had baptized 382 children, of whom 51 were black. While masters and mistresses had made "engagements for some . . . others had God fathers and God mothers of their own color" as they formerly had been baptized.

Despite Anglican efforts, the Baptists and Methodists proved most successful in conveying the Christian gospel to African Americans. The Methodists organized so late in the colonial era, however, that their influence was felt more during and after the Revolution. In their democratic approach to religion the Baptists encouraged blacks to participate fully in worship. Testimonies, baptisms, and disciplinary actions for whites and blacks alike occurred in common. Anglican minister John Barnett, writing from St. Philip's Parish in Brunswick County in 1766, not only believed that "New light baptists" were numerous in the parish but that "The most illiterate among them are their Teachers[;] even Negroes speak in their Meetings."

Quakers were the first sect to try to put their religious principles into practice and alter the slaves' status. Quakers owned slaves during the colonial period but became increasingly uneasy about the practice. At their monthly, quarterly, and annual meetings they began to question the treatment received by slaves of Friends, the necessity of buying and selling slaves by Friends, and in 1769 the desirability of owning slaves. In 1776, when white Americans launched their attempt to free themselves from their yoke of slavery to King George III, Quakers in North Carolina upheld the spirit of emancipation by announcing their intention to free their black slaves.

Attempts to convert Native Americans were less successful. Early Anglican missionaries spoke of meetings with the Indians and their chiefs. While some seemed amenable to conversion to Christianity, there is little indication of the widespread acceptance of Christianity by the Indians. Most of the English interest in Native Americans consisted of the efforts to combat the influence of the French and Catholicism along the frontier. Perhaps the most notable contribution on the part of whites was made by the Reverend Alexander Stewart who preached to the remnants of the Mattamuskeet, Roanoke, and Hatteras Indians in the Hyde County area. He baptized twenty-one Indians on one occasion and established a school for the Indians and blacks in the area.

Although the missionary impulse was a stimulus to the colonization of English America, whites experienced difficulty in their desire to Christianize Native Americans. Unlike blacks, Indians presented an element of militant opposition, more particularly when they colluded with the French. The English settlers found it easier to call the Indians a heathen people and wage war against them. The exceptions to this observation were those Native Americans to whom Stewart ministered, Indians who were effectively settled on reservations and presented no threat to whites.

In addition to the attempts of clergymen to minister to the needs of the people, the efforts of individual lay Christians should not be overlooked. Sincere Christians supported their churches and parishes with their time, effort, and money. At his death Gov. Henderson Walker left funds for the construction of a church and ten barrels of corn to be distributed equally among ten poor people in his area. Wilmington merchant John Paine ordered his executors to pay thirteen pounds to the churchwardens in each county in the province for the benefit of the poor. Others left money for the construction of churches both in North Carolina and in their native European countries, such as Ireland and Scotland. The most munificent gift was Alexander Duncan's bequest of four hundred pounds for finishing or adorning St. James Church in Wilmington. Clearly, religion was not defunct in the colony. North Carolinians had made remarkable progress in the realization of the benefits of organized religion in the century preceding the Revolution.

# CHAPTER SEVEN

# TRANSPORTATION AND COMMUNICATION

Transportation in colonial North Carolina was often slow, difficult, and hazardous. The early settlers found that the numerous swamps and general sparseness of population hindered the construction and maintenance of suitable highways in the province. Thus in the seventeenth and early eighteenth centuries the colonials depended greatly upon streams, creeks, rivers, and sounds for conveyance. Settlers purchased land on these waterways for purposes of personal travel and the transportation of agricultural produce. Private and public landings dotted the major creeks and rivers in the colony.

Carolinians used various types of boats to ply their inland waterways. Canoes were a popular and versatile craft. Generally made of cypress, the canoes varied in size from those that carried only one or two passengers to those that transported two or three horses. Smaller canoes were propelled by paddles or oars, while larger ones might be equipped with sails. Dr. John Brickell found that "no Boat in the World is capable to be rowed as fast as they are, and when they are full of Water they will not sink. . . ."

Piraguas, larger than canoes, were made from hollowed cypress logs that were widened by splitting the logs to add one or more planks. Oars and sails propelled these boats, which could transport as many as one hundred barrels of pitch and tar or several horses. Early in the colonial era the provincials used piraguas in the coastal trade, but after 1750 larger, more seaworthy vessels replaced them. Brickell observed that no European boat of the same size could outsail a Carolina piragua.

Carolinians also used various other boats for water transportation. Scows and flats were flat-bottomed, shallow-draft vessels designed principally for inland commerce. Small sloops or shallops were employed on the sounds and large rivers, though such craft were reported as far inland as Halifax on the Roanoke River in 1774. Yawls and bay boats occasionally appeared on the inland waters along with pleasure craft, such as the boat, complete with awnings and six uniformed slaves, which conveyed Janet Schaw down the Northeast Cape Fear to Wilmington.

As the sites along the waterways were preempted and the inhabitants of the province moved inland, more and better roads became mandatory. At first, many of the routes were constructed simply to connect interior plantations to public landings, but eventually roads were necessary for various aspects of intracounty transportation. Intracounty roads soon gave way to intercounty highways as a provincial road network emerged. By 1775 maps of North Carolina indicated an intricate transportation system, wherein the longer routes were connected by innumerable shorter roads.

Authorization for the construction of roads emanated from the provincial assembly and the various county courts. The few roads projected by the legislature were designed to facilitate intercounty travel, particularly for purposes of promoting trade. The county courts supervised the building of the vast majority of provincial highways. Generally, the justices entertained petitions from county residents for roads to public landings, churches, schools, courthouses, and mills. If the courts approved such petitions, as they usually did, they appointed twelve men to mark the proposed route and designated certain residents of the area to clear and maintain the road. All able-bodied males, white and black, were responsible for the construction and repair of roads.

The most important provincial roads included the King's Highway, which passed through Edenton, Bath, New Bern, and Wilmington, and the inland variation of that route, which came from Virginia through Halifax and Tarboro to New Bern. In the west, major trading routes ran from the Wachovia tract to Petersburg, Virginia, and to Charleston, South Carolina. The principal east-west roads passed from

New Bern, Wilmington, and Cross Creek to the western counties of Guilford, Rowan, and Mecklenburg. Countless shorter roads connected the major highways and intercounty routes.

Special types of construction were used for some of the shorter roads. Bridle roads, bridle paths, or "by-ways," narrower than the regularly authorized roads, were commonly used to reduce the expense and time of clearing a road of normal width. These roads were designed to connect a person's house or mill with a main road, a landing with a main road, or as a means of joining two highways. Causeways or "causeys" were built across lowlands and swamps. Frequently they were also constructed at ferry landings. The colonials built causeways by placing logs in the direction of the road, covering them with dirt, and overlaying the whole with small pine trees, brush, and dirt again. Usually the causeways were higher in the center and tapered to the edges to ensure proper drainage of water.

North Carolina roads were exceptionally narrow by European standards and rarely failed to register a negative impression on foreign travelers. An exception was the highway north of Wilmington leading to the Northeast Cape Fear River, which was wide enough for fifty men to march abreast, according to a Scottish visitor to the area. Many roads, however, were little more than blazed paths through the woods. The blazes or notches on the sides of the trees became difficult to discern after a number of years. The fact that many roads were barely distinguishable from animal paths and Indian paths compounded the traveler's woes. Guides were often necessary, though early in the colonial era it was common for guides to lose their way.

In 1764 the assembly ordered that the major roads in the province be posted and measured. The appearance of "Five Mile" posts and "Three Fingers" posts along the roads attested to at least partial compliance with the law. One traveler who rode from Bath to New Bern commented on the signposts with the number of miles marked in roman numerals and notches, the latter, he supposed, for the benefit of the unlearned. Despite the assistance of signposts and markers, many lost their way. One man spent the night in the woods between Brunswick and Wilmington fending off wolves. Another who became lost in the same area after taking a shortcut noted in a very positive manner in his journal never to take any more shortcuts in North Carolina.

Although the fortunate traveler might stay on the road, a satisfactory trip was not thereby ensured. In the eastern counties the roads often consisted of deep, loose, white sand, which slowed travel and tired horses. Occasionally the sand concealed tree roots that tripped horses. The traveler also feared the many dead trees lining the roadsides that could fall with thundering crashes during strong winds. This threat was the result of the colonial practices of boxing pines to obtain turpentine and burning forests to clear land.

Travel through North Carolina proved lonely, dull, and annoying at times. One could ride an entire day without meeting anyone or seeing a house. A traveler once commented that "Nothing can be more dreary, melancholy and uncomfortable than the almost perpetual solitary dreary pines, sandy barrens, and dismal swamps" throughout eastern North Carolina. That tiresome, unvaried scene was sometimes interrupted by frightening encounters with numerous snakes and by pesky mosquitoes.

The principal mode of transportation was the horse. It was said that the colonial would gladly walk five miles to catch his horse even for a ride of only one mile. The necessity for walking such a distance, if that was the case, stemmed from the fact that Carolinians often bestowed little care on their horses. They allowed the animals to roam loose in the woods and forage for themselves. Bishop August Spangenberg observed that at the end of the winter the horses were so emaciated they were of little benefit to their owners during the spring and summer.

Travel by horse was certainly the most rapid means of transportation. An average of thirty miles per day was considered a satisfactory journey. However, a rider might attempt fifty miles in a day, though he and his horse would be greatly fatigued by such a trip. In 1779 Whitmill Hill, a delegate to the Continental Congress from North Carolina, traversed the distance from Philadelphia to his home in Martin County in the remarkable time of seven and one-half days.

For transporting all but the lightest commodities a wagon or cart was necessary. Wagons were less numerous than carts and seemed to have been used mostly in the backcountry. Two or four horses pulled the wagons, which could carry an average load of two thousand pounds. Wagons proved indispensable for trading and mercantile operations in the Piedmont. The Moravians carried on an extensive trade with Charleston, Brunswick, New Bern, and Petersburg with such vehicles. Wagons also brought countless immigrants from the northern colonies and South Carolina into western North Carolina.

The cart was the predominant work vehicle throughout the colony. On the short-bodied, two-wheeled cart the planter could haul his produce to market, grain and fodder around the farm, and his family to church. So valuable was the cart that even the wheels were saved when the body was discarded. Such vehicles could carry average loads of one thousand pounds.

The high cost of some types of wheeled vehicles restricted ownership to the wealthy. The sulky and gig were light, one-passenger carriages; the chair and chaise, light, two-passenger carriages with two or four wheels; the post chaise, a four-wheeled chaise; the chariot, similar to the post chaise but having a coach box; the phaeton, a light, open, four-wheeled carriage; and the coach, a large, closed, four-wheeled carriage. The sulky and chair were the most prevalent wheeled carriages and could travel almost as fast as a horseman on the better roads of the province. The poor condition of most roads, however, discouraged the use of such vehicles until approximately two decades before the Revolution. Actually, few Carolinians traveled great distances anyway. Most limited their trips to visiting neighbors, going to church, hauling produce or driving livestock to market, and going to the courthouse on public occasions. Only the wealthier planters, merchants, lawyers, judges, assemblymen, clergymen, and itinerant peddlers traveled extensively.

The numerous streams, creeks, and rivers in the colony necessitated crossings by means of fords, bridges, and ferries. Narrower and shallower waters in the backcountry made fording easier in the Piedmont than along the coast where "impenetrable swamps and bottomless morasses" hindered such activities. Fords were natural crossings for roads, and a few fords were eventually bridged to eliminate the inconvenience of wading or swimming through waters with animals, carts, and wagons. Bridges were also constructed at private docks or landings, mills, and ferry sites to replace ferries.

Provincial legislation provided general instructions for the building of bridges, and the county courts added the details. A typical bridge was at least twelve feet wide and about five to seven feet above the water. It consisted of fifteen-inch pilings driven into the stream bed.

Sills or sleepers were set into them and braced with timbers seven by five inches thick. The floor was made of sawed boards, "clear of sap" and at least two inches thick. The bridge had one or two protective rails on each side, which were three by four inches thick. Cypress was used extensively for bridge construction in the eastern counties. If a bridge survived the frequent floods, or freshets as they were called, its average lifetime was ten to fifteen years.

The men who constructed and repaired the roads also built the bridges. In 1745, however, the legislature permitted some counties to contract with private individuals to build bridges at the expense of the county taxpayers. Later this privilege was extended to all the counties in the province. Often the county courts required the contractors to keep bridges repaired for as many as seven years after the structures were completed. The cost of erecting such bridges ranged from only £4 for one over a small stream in Bute County to the large sum of £190 for the bridge over the Tar River at Tarboro in Edgecombe County, which was one of the most impressive bridges in the colony.

Private toll bridges supplemented the public facilities. On rare occasions the assembly authorized individuals to construct bridges and charge travelers stipulated rates for the use of the bridges. Cumberland County also followed that practice. The county court permitted the private bridge keepers to charge the same rates as ferry operators but demanded that persons on public business be allowed to pass free of charge.

At least two drawbridges, a type of bridge construction which was rare in colonial America, were located in North Carolina. The oldest and best known was that of Capt. Benjamin Heron, who was authorized by the assembly to build a drawbridge over the Northeast Cape Fear just north of present Castle Hayne. Heron's bridge opened in the middle by a system of pulleys. The other drawbridge was constructed over the Cashie River at Windsor in Bertie County by order of the Bertie County court. Prominent residents of New Bern and Craven County attempted to raise enough money by private subscriptions to build a drawbridge over the Trent River at Swimming Point, but the Revolution interrupted their efforts.

Where fords and bridges were inadequate to cross watercourses, the colonials resorted to ferries. A scattered population and restricted mobility resulting from poor roads retarded the development of ferry service in North Carolina. There appears to have been no regular ferriage from Edenton across the Albemarle Sound as late as 1745. By the 1760s, however, ferry service had been established throughout the eastern counties.

The more westerly counties had less need of ferriage since their waters could often be forded or bridged. Still, the Northeast Cape Fear, Tar, Haw, Catawba, and Yadkin Rivers required ferry crossings, and the establishment of ferries was of prime concern to people living near those rivers. By the end of the colonial period, North Carolina probably possessed a sufficient number of ferries for its transportation network, though the quality of ferriage service may have been questionable.

The creation of ferries proceeded principally from two sources of authority—the provincial assembly and the county courts. The county courts issued most of the ferry licenses. When authorizing ferry service, the courts determined the location of the ferry, the boats required for transport, rates charged for passage, and bonds for ensuring the proper performance of duties by ferry keepers. Boats used for ferriage included canoes, piraguas, flats, and scows. Along the coast these vessels were usually in poor condition. The one on the Neuse River at New Bern was once described as "very bad." At Sneads Ferry over New River the boat was an "ordinary bauble" that floated no more than two or three inches above the water. William Dry's boats on either side of Eagles Island in the Cape Fear, opposite Wilmington, were leaky craft in which passengers were often soaked while crossing the river.

In addition to boats, some ferry keepers kept pastures where horses could graze while the animals and their owners awaited passage. The New Hanover County court in 1760 ordered all ferrymen in the county to furnish pens or pounds for detaining cattle and forcing them into the water. Late in the colonial period consideration was given to the owners of these animals. The assembly required ferry keepers at the longer ferriage points to maintain taverns so that travelers might refresh themselves as they waited.

Delays at ferries were common. If the ferryboat was on the opposite bank, the prospective passenger gave notice of his presence by ringing a bell provided for that purpose or by yelling across the water. Yet, service was not always forthcoming. Ebenezer Hazard once found that the ferryman at Bath had "run away." And the weather compounded the errors of man. Adverse winds and waters might delay passage at the wider ferries—such as the Albemarle Sound crossing—for two or three days. The Reverend Joseph Pilmore recorded his detention on Eagles Island during a thunderstorm in March 1773. He feared that he might have to spend the night on the island, but the storm abated late in the afternoon allowing him to shout for the boat in Wilmington.

The legislature gave impetus to public transportation in North Carolina in 1741 by instituting a system of free ferriage for persons traveling across New River from White House Point to Johnston, the newly created town and county seat of Onslow County. The free ferry proved so advantageous that the court continued the practice after the county seat was moved to Wantland's Ferry (now Jacksonville). The assembly followed the Johnston experiment with legislation in 1754 and 1758 establishing free ferries across the Perquimans and Pasquotank Rivers to facilitate travel to and from the county courthouses during court sessions, the election of members of the vestry and assembly, and the gathering of musters. Eventually the counties of Hertford, Rowan, Mecklenburg, Pitt, Tyrrell, and Anson were permitted to establish free ferry transportation. At least two counties, Cumberland and Bertie, also supervised the operation of ferries at public expense but without legislative authorization.

The ferries often adversely affected communications in the colony. Coupled with the poor quality of many of the roads, the longer ferries at Edenton, Bath, New Bern, and Wilmington proved to be obstacles to the establishment of regular postal service in North Carolina. Ferries also detained members of the assembly, which obstructed legislative business and possibly determined the contest for Speaker of the house in 1754. Chief Justice Martin Howard noted that the "many wide and dangerous ferrys" hampered the administration of justice and helped make his office more burdensome and expensive than any on the continent. The ferries also hindered the ministerial activities of the many itinerant preachers in the colony.

Communication in colonial North Carolina rested heavily upon oral transmission. Illiteracy, transportation difficulties, and inadequate postal facilities prevented widespread reliance upon the written word.

The tradition of southern hospitality stemmed in part from the desire for good conversation and news from the outside world. Travelers of the upper class were eagerly sought by their counterparts in North Carolina. Hosts pleaded with their guests to remain for weeks while they plied their visitors for the latest international and intercolonial developments.

The lower classes were not unfriendly. In fact, a marked characteristic of all such American colonials was their inordinate curiosity. To upper- or middle-class travelers such inquisitiveness bordered on impertinence, but actually it was the result of a desire for information about the external world. Many colonials traveled no more than fifty miles from their place of birth during their lifetime. Some were so ignorant that they could not have named the reigning monarchs of England.

Written communications consisted principally of letters and newspapers. Lacking other means of communication, colonials became adept and comprehensive letter writers. The techniques of writing and the art of calligraphy were more highly developed than in the twentieth century, and the correspondents included far more general news than modern composers of letters. When Peter DuBois of Wilmington wrote to his friend Samuel Johnston of Edenton in 1757, he observed that two English squadrons were outfitting for a secret mission, that the Russians had been denied a passage through Poland, that the king of Prussia remained firm in his alliance, that the Byng trial had begun in England, and that Parliament intended to impeach several highly placed officials.

Newspapers were an important channel of communication in the colonial era, but North Carolina was one of the last colonies to benefit from this medium of information. The first paper, the *North Carolina Gazette*, was published in New Bern in 1751. Thereafter the *North Carolina Magazine; or, Universal Intelligencer* (New Bern), the *North Carolina Gazette and Weekly Post Boy* (Wilmington), and the *Cape Fear Mercury* (Wilmington) served the colony before the Revolution. These papers carried mostly international news with small amounts of intercolonial and local material. Of course, the releases were dated. Three to ten months elapsed between the occurrence of events in the northern colonies or England and the reports in North Carolina newspapers. Nevertheless, the papers were eagerly awaited by the provincials, who scrutinized their contents, read them to the less literate, and gave them to friends and acquaintances. Thus, newspapers probably reached an audience that was four to five times the number of subscribers.

The lack of an adequate postal system before the Revolution accounted in part for the difficulty of communications in the colony. Only in 1770 was a regular postal service realized. Before 1770 Carolinians relied upon friends, expresses (private carriers), and packet boats in the coastal trade to transport letters and papers. Expresses were expensive, and their cost deterred sending all but important correspondence by that means. The alternatives, however, were generally slower and less reliable than expresses.

Gov. William Tryon was responsible for the creation of a systematic postal service for the colony. When he succeeded Gov. Arthur Dobbs in 1765 North Carolina was the only English province along the seaboard that lacked postal facilities. A gap existed in postal communications from Suffolk, Virginia, to Charleston, South Carolina. Vigorous prodding of the North Carolina assembly and frequent correspondence with the governors of Virginia and South Carolina and British postal authorities produced sufficient money and cooperation to open a postal route through North Carolina to connect Suffolk and Charleston.

Still, by 1774 there was only one post road in the province. It passed through Edenton, Bath, New Bern, and Wilmington. Poor roads and long ferriages across the Albemarle Sound and Pamlico River hindered the postriders who carried the mail each way every two weeks. The postmasters in the towns were unreliable and failed to maintain regular post offices. Letters were carelessly tossed on tables or floors with no regard for the security of the correspondence. Frequently the mail was lost or opened by other parties.

British postal inspector Hugh Finlay spent three months in North Carolina in 1774 attempting to correct the inadequacies of the service. He chastised negligent postmasters and instructed riders in their duties. Finlay arranged for a post office in Brunswick, regular service between Wilmington and Brunswick, and a post between Wilmington and Cross Creek (now Fayetteville), the first east-west route in the province. Nevertheless, on the eve of the Revolution postal service was slow, unreliable, and inefficient. For that matter, so was communication in North Carolina in general.

The absence of a postal system for so much of the colonial period highlighted the relative isolation of North Carolina along the Atlantic coast. True, the colony soon developed an oceangoing trade as New Englanders sailed to the Albemarle in the seventeenth century for tobacco and wheat. Later, stock raisers drove cattle to market as far away as New Jersey. The Moravians maintained close contact with Pennsylvania and undertook to sell their goods in Charleston, South Carolina. Still, the absence of a regular post, lack of satisfactory intercolonial highways, and a dangerous coast made communication with the world beyond North Carolina difficult.

North Carolina's ocean traffic was conducted in schooners, sloops, brigs, ships, and snows. The small schooners and sloops were utilized in the coastal trade with other colonies; brigs, or brigantines, for the West Indies; the larger ships and snows, for transoceanic voyages to England and Europe. The length of a voyage depended not only upon the distance to be traversed but upon many other factors, such as the weather, size of the vessel, weight of cargo, and skill of the captain and crew. To venture from Wilmington to Charleston, South Carolina, in 1735 took two days. Just before the Revolution a trip from New York to Cape Lookout required nine days; a sail to the West Indies, slightly less than two weeks; a transatlantic crossing, as little as three weeks but more likely seven to eight weeks.

Water proved easier and quicker than overland communication to other provinces along the coast. The Dismal Swamp hindered travel to Virginia; Carolina bays obstructed travel to the south. News of the Battle of Lexington in Massachusetts in 1775 took nine days by land to reach North Carolina. Even after the advent of a formal postal system, postriders in 1774 needed twenty-seven days to carry a letter from Charleston, South Carolina, through North Carolina to Suffolk, Virginia, an average of sixteen miles a day. And communication was no faster within North Carolina—in 1773 a letter written in New Bern and carried by a traveler to the Moravians in Wachovia took two weeks to reach its destination.

Isolation not only affected life in the province but the mentality of North Carolinians. Positively, it may have contributed to a spirit of self-reliance and independence on the part of the people. However, business generally, and merchants in particular, suffered from a lack of ready knowledge about prices and markets. Ignorance led to rumormongering, especially during wartime, and needed, accurate information was hard to obtain. Moreover, isolation bred provincialism and a narrowness of vision, which may have contributed to North Carolina's reluctance to ratify immediately the federal constitution after the Revolutionary War.

CHAPTER EIGHT

# TOWN LIFE

Urbanization proceeded very slowly in North Carolina, though the proprietors and the Crown encouraged the formation of towns. The governing authorities valued urban communities as fortresses to protect surrounding settlements and as centers of trade and culture. By the time of the Revolution, however, only about 2 percent of North Carolina's population, or perhaps five thousand people, lived in urban areas. Compared with other British American colonies, North Carolina was slightly less urbanized, and its largest towns did not remotely approximate the populations of Philadelphia, New York, Boston, or Charleston. Indeed, North Carolina remained a distinctly rural colony.

The towns of North Carolina developed in response to the demands of trade and commerce. In the east they were situated on the best harbor sites in order to take advantage of maritime commerce. In the interior, towns appeared on the principal trading routes, especially at the intersections of such thoroughfares, or served as intermediary junctions between western and eastern towns. Despite the small number of towns and the paucity of urban residents, the importance of these settlements should not be underestimated. They performed an inestimable role in the economic development of the colony.

The oldest town in the province was Bath, which was incorporated in 1705/06, a half century after the permanent settlement of North Carolina. Bath probably contained no more than thirty houses during the colonial period. Although the town was an official port of entry, its commercial importance was limited. Nevertheless, it impressed travelers as a "pretty little place" and contained acceptable lodging facilities. Among the early and occasional residents of Bath was the notorious pirate Edward Teach, alias Blackbeard, who was killed off the North Carolina coast in 1718.

Beaufort, settled about 1710 and incorporated in 1723, also remained relatively insignificant during the colonial period. It too was a port of entry but handled little commerce because of its shallow harbor and its inability to tap inland trade. In 1765 a traveler noted that there were no more than twelve houses in Beaufort. The people appeared indolent and subsisted primarily on the abundant fish and oysters found in the area. But during the next ten years Beaufort enjoyed a surge of growth, and in the early 1770s there were at least sixty families living in the town.

Edenton was one of the most pleasant and beautiful towns in the province. Located on the northwestern end of the Albemarle Sound and named for Gov. Charles Eden, the town contained some 160 houses and one thousand inhabitants at the time of the Revolution. During the first part of the colonial era, the legislature met regularly in the town, and the governors kept residences there. Later Edenton served as the county seat of Chowan County and the location of Lord Granville's land office. It was also a major port. Trade was conducted primarily with the coastal areas and West Indies. Although Edenton and the Albemarle area were nominally part of North Carolina, the long ferriage over the Albemarle Sound and the poor road facilities tended to isolate the region from the rest of the colony. In fact, before the Revolution the northeastern counties of North Carolina appear to have maintained closer social and commercial ties to Virginia.

New Bern, founded by Christoph von Graffenried in 1710 at the confluence of the Neuse and Trent Rivers, rivaled Wilmington as the largest urban center in the colony by 1775. New Bern developed slowly at first; in 1745 it was no larger than Bath. But by 1765, the town comprised some one hundred buildings and five hundred people. It continued to increase in population and size, and by the outbreak of the Revolution encompassed a larger geographic area than any other town in the colony.

Blackbeard the Pirate, also called Edward Teach, tied his long beard in pigtails and wore burning fuses sticking out from under his hat in order to frighten his victims. He lived for a time in Bath, North Carolina, and often operated at Ocracoke Inlet. Blackbeard was killed near Ocracoke Island in 1718 by Lt. Robert Maynard, who had come searching for the pirate at the behest of the governor of Virginia. Picture from the files of the Division of Archives and History.

New Bern's rapid growth resulted from an influx of enterprising merchants in the 1760s who began to draw on the interior trade of the colony. Even the Moravians occasionally sent goods to sale in the town. The central coastal location of New Bern eventually led to its selection as the capital of the province, and the permanent placement of government offices and officers in the town further enhanced the commercial possibilities of the area. Although much of New Bern's growth was expansion in the absolute sense, some of it came at the expense of Bath and Beaufort.

In the southeast, Brunswick and Wilmington vied for supremacy as commercial centers. Brunswick was founded in 1726 in the process of the settlement of the Cape Fear by the Moore brothers. Beautifully situated high on the west bank of the Cape Fear River and offering the best port facilities in the province, Brunswick should have been in a position to monopolize the river trade. The Moore family and their allies were opposed in the 1730s, however, by a political faction that included Gov. Gabriel Johnston, who sponsored the establishment of Wilmington to contest Brunswick's early primacy.

Johnston and his cohorts succeeded in reducing Brunswick to a state of relative unimportance. Wilmington expanded rapidly while Brunswick languished. Nevertheless, Brunswick maintained a continuous existence throughout the colonial period. Governors Dobbs and Tryon established their residences at Russellborough, just north of Brunswick, until 1771 when Tryon moved to his "palace" in New Bern. In addition, the "flats," a shallow sandbar across the Cape Fear River above Brunswick and below Wilmington, prevented large transatlantic vessels from calling at Wilmington without lightering. As a result, some captains preferred to unload their entire cargoes at Brunswick. Thus a corps of merchants and royal customs officials resided in the town to avail themselves of this business. On the eve of the Revolution, Brunswick may have contained as many as fifty buildings, but one visitor described it as "very poor—a few scattered houses on the edge of the woods, without street or regularity." During the Revolution the British raided the lower Cape Fear area, and the inhabitants of Brunswick abandoned the town.

Wilmington flourished from its inception to become one of the most populous towns in the province. Known as New Carthage, New Liverpool, and Newton, Wilmington thrived under the promotion of

The ruins of St. Philips Church, at one time the largest church in the colony, stand at Brunswick Town State Historic Site. During the Revolution Brunswick was abandoned by its residents and burned by the British. Photograph from the files of the Division of Archives and History.

the provincial governors. It eventually contained 150 to 200 houses. Wilmington owed its importance to its port facilities and its partially successful effort to divert the backcountry trade from Charleston. Numerous Scottish and Scotch-Irish merchants settled in Wilmington and helped to build the town into the most active commercial center in North Carolina before the Revolution.

The middle portion of the province contained the towns of Halifax, Tarboro, Cross Creek, and Campbellton. Halifax was founded in 1757 at the instigation of several merchants who desired to take advantage of the commercial possibilities offered by the Roanoke River traffic. Settlement was delayed slightly by a smallpox epidemic about 1758, but eventually the town contained approximately fifty houses, which were mostly of wood or frame construction and painted white. Tarboro was established in 1760 on the Tar River, principally to provide Edgecombe County with a satisfactory county seat. Although Tarboro served as a mercantile center, it grew slowly and had only half the population of Halifax.

Present Fayetteville was the product of two towns that originated in the colonial period. Cross Creek, situated on a tributary of the Northwest Cape Fear by that name, materialized in the 1750s to divert trade from the backcountry to the eastern coast. The naturalist William Bartram, in his vivid account of the town, described Cross Creek as being

on some heights or swelling hills, from whence the creek descends precipitately, then gently meanders near a mile . . . to its confluence with the river [where men] built mills, which drew people to the place who exercised mechanic arts, as smiths, wheelwrights, carpenters, coopers, tanners, etc. And at length merchants were encouraged to adventure and settle; in short, within eight or ten years from a grist-mill, saw-mill, smith-shop and a tavern, arose a flourishing commercial town.

The success of Cross Creek spurred a group of men to attempt the establishment of a competing settlement on the river approximately a mile away. In 1762 the assembly incorporated the latter town, and it was called Campbellton. In 1778 both towns were merged under the name Campbellton, which later was changed to Fayetteville.

Western towns included Hillsborough, Salisbury, Salem, and Charlotte. Hillsborough, called Corbinton and Childsburgh until its incorporation as Hillsborough in 1766, was the county seat of Orange County and was situated on the "Western Path" or "Indian Trading Path," once an important route for trade conducted by the Catawba and Cherokee Indians. In 1764 the town contained thirty to forty permanent residents, among them tavern keepers, merchants, and lawyers. Public buildings included a courthouse, jail, and church.

Salisbury, also situated on the Trading Path as well as on the Great Wagon Road from Pennsylvania, was the county seat of Rowan County. Although larger than Hillsborough, Salisbury was smaller than Halifax. After its formal creation in 1755, diverse tradesmen established businesses in the town. Within ten years a candlemaker, a doctor, two lawyers, a potter, three hatters, a weaver, a tailor, a butcher, an Indian trader, and a wagonmaker, accompanied by numerous tavern keepers, had settled in Salisbury. Despite this thriving atmosphere, the commerce of Salisbury was distinctly secondary to that of Hillsborough.

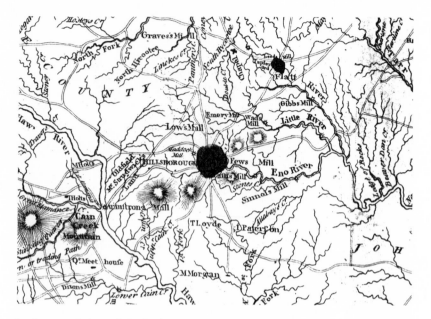

As the population of the backcountry increased during the latter stages of the colonial era, towns such as Hillsborough were established. This section of "A Compleat Map of North Carolina from an actual Survey" by John Collet, published in 1770, shows Hillsborough and its environs.

The Moravians founded Salem in 1766 to serve as the urban center of Wachovia. It was preceded, however, by two smaller towns, Bethabara and Bethania, which were laid out in 1753 and 1759, respectively. For the most part Bethabara contained tradesmen—tailors, shoemakers, carpenters, potters, tanners, millwrights, and gunsmiths—while Bethania was a farming community. By 1766 Bethabara contained eighty-eight inhabitants and Bethania seventy-eight.

Salem evolved from the usual thoroughness of the Moravians who carefully selected a site and planned the settlement of their town. The Moravians more than any other settlers meticulously calculated their economic activities and systematically sought the most lucrative commercial markets for their products. The busiest institutions in and around Salem were the pottery, store, tavern, gristmill, and sawmill. The town was an immediate commercial success; it served much of the backcountry of North Carolina, including Native Americans who frequently enjoyed the magnanimous hospitality offered by the Moravians.

Charlotte, currently the largest city in North Carolina, had an inauspicious beginning. An act of the provincial assembly in 1768 created the town, which the legislature hoped would become another center of trade in the backcountry. Although designated the county seat of Mecklenburg County and the site of Queen's College, Charlotte grew slowly. William Moultrie, a South Carolina surveyor, visited the town in 1772 and found a courthouse, jail, tavern, and five or six houses. The importance of the town had yet to materialize.

In addition to these commercial centers of urban development, North Carolina also possessed a complement of smaller, less influential towns. Several were intended as county seats and still exercise that function today—Hertford in Perquimans County, Kinston in Lenoir, Winton in Hertford, Windsor in Bertie, and Elizabethtown in Bladen. Nixonton, in Pasquotank County, was incorporated as a county seat but subsequently lost that distinction. It was, however, a sizable village even at its formal establishment in 1758. Some twenty houses had been built, and seventy people resided in the area at that time.

A few towns founded in the colonial period either failed or ceased to function. Some were paper communities, like Wimberly in Bertie County in 1752, which were authorized by statute but never surveyed and occupied. Johnston, at Mittam's Point on the south side of New River in Onslow County, was incorporated in 1741 but was demolished by a hurricane in 1752 and thereafter abandoned. Portsmouth, established in 1753 near Ocracoke Inlet in Carteret County, was designed as a commercial community to cater to shipping in the Pamlico Sound area. Though a thriving village at one time, the Civil War contributed to its decline, and by the late twentieth century Portsmouth had virtually been abandoned.

The North Carolina legislature in chartering towns used the commission form of government for directing local affairs. In many instances the commissioners were self-perpetuating (Edenton, 1722; Halifax, 1757; Windsor, 1767), but in some instances the justices of the county courts in whose jurisdiction the towns lay cooperated with the remaining commissioners to appoint replacements for commissioners who had died or moved (Woodstock, 1738; Beaufort, 1770; Salisbury, 1770). In the cases of Wilmington (1745), New Bern (1748), and Brunswick (1767), the legislature allowed qualified townspeople to elect their commissioners.

A brief aberration in town governance occurred in the 1760s, when Gov. Arthur Dobbs introduced the municipal corporation, or borough, common in England and in some northern colonies. Corporation government consisted of a mayor, borough recorder, and aldermen. Wilmington received a municipal charter from the governor in 1760, as did New Bern, Halifax, and Edenton. By 1768, however, Wilmington and the other towns had returned to the commission system, perhaps because the commission was simpler and provided more flexibility of governance than the municipal corporation.

However, when the townspeople of Wilmington formally surrendered their charter to Gov. Josiah Martin in 1773, they voiced their hope that "His Majesty may grant us another Charter of Incorporation free from the defects and inconveniences" of the present document. The principal objections to the charter included vague borough boundaries, an inordinately large number of aldermen relative to the number of townspeople, and the requirement that all town residents meet periodically as a common council to enact ordinances and bylaws, which inconvenienced "industrious Tradesmen." The petitioners suggested delineating the bounds of the borough more carefully, reducing the number of aldermen, and electing a common council annually so that the people could "take the Burthen [of governing] alternately." Wilmington's citizens, at least, apparently favored a borough government that included features of the commission system.

Urban conditions in colonial North Carolina are best revealed by *The Wilmington Town Book*, a 1973 published edition of the meetings of the town officials of Wilmington between 1743 and 1778. After the election of the town commissioners by the freeholders, the first order of business in 1743 was to agree to a resurvey of the town lots in order to settle disputes over property boundaries. North Carolinians were a particularly litigious people who happily, it seemed, quarreled over boundary lines and any other matters in urban as well as rural areas. And Wilmington was representative of other towns, such as Beaufort, which also required periodic assessments of town boundaries.

Still, Wilmington citizens continued to disregard property lines. Dr. Moses John DeRosset later complained that James Campbell refused to move his billiard house which was on DeRosset's land. In 1772 the town commissioners issued a list of fifty-eight houses and businesses whose piazzas, balconies, steps, and other structures encroached upon the streets. These included George Moore's stable and poultry house, John Burgwin's tar shed, and John Lyon's tannery. The commissioners imposed an annual rent on all those buildings that interfered with the public right-of-way.

Proper use of municipal property, particularly on the waterfront, concerned town commissioners. Bath initially sought to preserve the beauty of the town by prohibiting wharf construction and preventing obstructions of the view of the water. In 1723, however, it relented and, like other towns, encouraged commerce by permitting wharves and warehouses. Wilmington commissioners undertook the construction of public wharves in 1749 and 1752 and contracted for the construction of a boat slip at the Market Street wharf in 1772. Periodically the commissioners called upon the adult males of the town to make and maintain those structures.

Wilmington residents faced the constant problem of construction and maintenance of streets, alleys, and docks. Twice a year the commissioners demanded that all adult males, including slaves, meet to effect the necessary construction and repairs. In this respect Wilmington was representative of most North Carolina towns. Yet, the city had a peculiar difficulty in that it was surrounded by sand hills and numerous streams flowed through the town. Drainage proved a constant problem, and the people of Wilmington bore the burden of building bridges in their town.

The men of Wilmington seem to have habitually avoided working on the streets. The town commissioners annually published long lists of defaulters, or those who failed to report for street work. These lists contained thirty to forty names and even included commissioners, such as John Rutherfurd, Caleb Mason, and Magnus Cowan, who set a poor example for the townspeople they supposedly served. Defaulters generally received opportunities to remove their obligations. If, however, they insisted on remaining delinquent, fines were imposed. Then another difficulty arose. Occasionally the constables who collected the fines found the sums tempting. At least two of those officers of the law absconded with their collections.

The people of Wilmington eventually relieved themselves of the drudgery of building bridges over the streams in the town. After 1772 the commissioners hired workers to construct drainage arches or tunnels of brick and timber over the streams and under the streets. The arches were approximately two feet wide and six and a half feet in height. Portions of these unusual tunnels still remain visible.

Despite the efforts to promote better drainage, Wilmington streets continued in a state of disrepair. In 1775 visitor Janet Schaw found the streets very muddy. And so it was with all North Carolina towns. Only the very large urban areas of the northern colonies—Boston, Newport, Philadelphia, and New York—had begun paving their streets before the Revolution.

The failure of Wilmington residents to care for the streets was not the only indication of indolence or lack of civic pride. Throughout the colonial era the commissioners passed ordinances to compel the inhabitants of the town to clear the streets, alleys, and docks of dirt, rubbish, and other nuisances. Whites were fined for breaking the law, whereas slaves were whipped for their offenses. By 1774 the town was sufficiently populous to justify the appointment of a town scavenger to clean the streets once a week. Apparently the office of trash collector was not wholly desirable. Three men held the position during 1774.

The growth of Wilmington from a village to a thriving urban center was reflected not only in the difficulties of street repair and trash removal but also in the problems of traffic control. Eventually ordinances were passed to prevent persons from riding "immoderately or uncommonly fast" through the streets, conducting races in the streets, and keeping "unruly horses" in the town. In the larger cities of the northern colonies, traffic accidents occasionally took the lives of innocent bystanders. Wilmington intended to protect its residents, and the commissioners often levied fines against the lawbreakers. Traffic problems were not unique to Wilmington. Salisbury also had difficulty with people driving wildly through its streets with unloaded carts and wagons, while the Carteret County court levied fines for racing in the streets of Beaufort.

The presence of livestock roaming the streets and yards of the towns continually evoked laws and ordinances to cope with the nuisance. Most of the regulations simply forbade hogs, goats, and other animals from running loose and imposed fines on their owners. Several towns, including Edenton, Bath, and New Bern, erected fences to prevent the intrusion of livestock from beyond the town limits. The fencing deteriorated quickly, however, and probably failed to serve its purpose.

Large urban communities also faced the constant threat of fire. Houses clustered together contributed to a rapid spread of flames, particularly when many of the buildings were frame with daub and wooden chimneys and wooden shingles. Such structures caught fire easily and blazed fiercely. Wilmington experienced at least five fires during the eighteenth century—in 1756, 1772, 1775, 1786, and 1798.

The danger of fire arose from many sources in Wilmington. Fires built on the wharves for boiling pitch and tar and on the streets for burning rubbish caused great concern. Eventually the commissioners banned such fires after sunset. They also ordered that all hay, straw, fodder, and oakum stored in residences be removed in hopes that the elimination of these flammable materials would reduce the risk of fire.

Sooty chimneys probably caused most of the fires in the town, and fire prevention centered on chimneys in the houses and kitchens. The commissioners required that all chimneys be at least three feet above the highest part of the roof so that sparks would be extinguished before settling on the roofs. Fines were imposed on people whose chimneys caught fire. The fines did not spur the townspeople to clean their chimneys, however, and the commissioners finally ordered all residents to sweep their chimneys from top to bottom every two weeks. Later, the time period for cleaning chimneys was extended to twenty days for kitchen fireplaces throughout the year and for all fireplaces between October and April. An attempt to hire a town chimney sweep failed. Furthermore, the regulations were ineffective, and fines continued to be imposed for chimney fires.

Wilmington also developed a program for fighting fires. Taxes were levied to purchase leather fire buckets and ladders for public use. The commissioners loaned these items to citizens for private use, and to their dismay the townspeople often failed to return them. Such negligence eventually evoked ordinances restricting the use of public property for private benefit. Additional laws required each housekeeper in Wilmington to purchase one or more water buckets, but again the townspeople ignored the law. The commissioners continually reminded the people to obtain the necessary fire buckets.

The preeminent piece of fire-fighting equipment in the town was the fire engine. A special property tax—as opposed to the usual poll tax—was placed on the houses in Wilmington for the purchase of the engine. The commissioners in 1755 engaged Benjamin Heron to procure the machine in London. The town had little need for the engine; this was fortunate since the equipment failed to receive the constant supervision and repair it needed. By 1772 the fire engine had so greatly deteriorated that the town decided to buy a newer, larger model. The commissioners intended to sell the older engine but later determined to have it repaired so that it would "throw water an equal distance of a New Engine." Within eighteen months the new engine had arrived from Philadelphia. Apparently neither of the fire engines was utilized to combat the 1775 fire.

Statutes relating to other towns in the province indicated a similar concern about fire hazards. For example, wooden chimneys were forbidden in Halifax and New Bern. In addition, the commissioners of Edenton received legislative approval in 1756 to levy a tax on town residents for the purchase of a fire engine. The Moravian records show that several small fires prompted the appointment of fire inspectors in Bethabara in 1759 and in Salem in 1773. The inhabitants of Bethabara regularly cleaned their chimneys during the years before the Revolution; Salem obtained the services of a chimney sweep.

The large slave populations of Wilmington and other coastal towns posed another concern to the white citizenry. The ability of bondsmen to rent houses and tenements or to obtain lodging in the towns evidenced an independence that was troublesome, if not dangerous. The Chowan County court eventually "Ordered that no Slave or Slaves shall be allowed to keep in [Edenton] any Houses, . . . it having been found by long experience that . . . suffering Slaves to keep Houses of their Own is a very great nuisance." Wilmington enacted ordinances to prevent slaves from renting houses, kitchens, and outbuildings, which tended "greatly to promote Idleness, Revelling and disturbance, Thieving and Stealing and many other crimes." Little substantive change followed these directives, however.

While some slaves used buildings belonging to their masters, others had sufficient funds to rent dwellings. They actively engaged in sundry trades, independent of the direction of their masters. This was done generally by working for others in their spare time. The resulting independent income provided slaves with a measure of freedom in a supposedly repressive environment. Wilmington ordinances show that blacks were buying, selling, and bartering firewood, provisions, and various types of merchandise.

Slaves certainly had considerable time to use at their discretion. They often gathered in the streets, alleys, and vacant lots or houses for convivial association. In New Bern in 1774 the town constable was ordered to take possession of the old jail and incarcerate disorderly slaves. Disturbances engendered by slaves constantly bothered inhabitants of Wilmington, and in 1772 such activities apparently led to the outbreak of a fire in the town. Reckless riding on horseback and racing in the streets by slaves elicited protest. Worse, however, was the potential threat posed by slaves after dark. Stealing, or even physical violence, was a danger in the unlighted streets of the town. Thus Wilmington imposed a curfew on slaves, exempting only those who possessed a pass from their masters and those who carried candles or lanterns.

The town ordinances, particularly those of Wilmington, generally failed to satisfy their intended purpose. Their lack of success derived principally from the failure of whites to support the regulations. The pecuniary motive seemed primarily responsible for the negligent enforcement of the ordinances. Whites rented unused tenements and outbuildings to slaves; they sold rum and other strong drink to bondsmen; they used the labor of skilled slaves, which could be obtained at low wages; they sold profitably goods that had been produced or stolen by slaves. Neither provincial legislation nor town action greatly discouraged the "pernicious practice of dealing with Negroes."

Another major concern in Wilmington was the sale of meat and produce. Originally the area below the courthouse served as the town marketplace, but during the 1740s a separate market house was constructed. In order to give all town residents an equal opportunity to purchase produce, the commissioners ordered that all goods be sold at the market house until 10 A.M. At that time they could be vended about the streets. The public received further protection through laws prohibiting the sale of unwholesome meat and diluted milk. Similar ordinances passed by the commissioners of New Bern showed equal concern for the public welfare. In New Bern retailers of grain, dairy, and poultry products were prohibited from buying in the market until nine o'clock so that housekeepers might have the first opportunity to purchase produce.

The variety of other matters that occupied the attention of the Wilmington town commissioners is intriguing. In 1752 several supposedly rabid dogs terrorized the inhabitants of the town; in 1763 materials were purchased to make a cushion and slipcover for the pulpit of St. James Church; in 1768 workers were hired to sink two wells near the courthouse for public use; in 1773 the commissioners rebuked the owners of open necessary houses that affronted the public; and in 1774 the town purchased a ducking stool (a device which Edenton had deemed necessary in 1767) for the punishment of prostitutes, gossips, scolds, and brawlers.

Although towns originated as places of trade, a purpose they fulfilled admirably, they quickly became the focus of political activity. The legislature convened in Bath, Edenton, New Bern, and Wilmington before it designated New Bern as the permanent capital of the colony in 1766. In keeping with the British tradition of recognizing the special interests of towns and according them representation in Parliament, North Carolina permitted its largest towns legislative representation in the colonial General Assembly.

The towns that served as county seats contained courthouses that attracted large numbers of people on public business, particularly on court days. Jails were built near the courthouses. In Wilmington in 1768, the jail lot was enclosed by a board fence "for a Garden for the benefit of the prisoners." Stocks, pillories, and whipping posts sometimes accompanied the jails.

Towns also served as social and cultural centers in early North Carolina. The clustering of people fostered organized religion, facilitated the formation of clubs, and provided an audience for literary publications. The strength of the Anglican Church in North Carolina lay in the coastal towns. Soon after the mid-eighteenth century the Masonic Order appeared in Wilmington, New Bern, and Halifax. Bookdealers opened shops in the larger towns, and New Bern and Wilmington witnessed the printing of the colony's four pre-Revolutionary newspapers.

Although the towns were relatively small, some, like Wilmington, became "places of elegance." A visitor to Wilmington in 1757 commented favorably on the houses, many of which were brick structures, two or three stories in height, with double piazzas. The more affluent residents enjoyed frequent visitors, hosted teas and dances, and in some instances formed dancing assemblies. Wealth also attracted itinerant professionals, including portrait painters who appealed to those willing and able to afford the luxury of leaving a likeness to posterity. Theatrical performers visited the coastal towns, perhaps as early as 1769, spurring in turn the creation of local thalian societies.

Towns in colonial North Carolina were urban centers in a rural landscape where one might travel for miles, even half a day or more, without encountering another person or even seeing a farmstead. And though they paled in comparison with European or more northerly colonial towns, the North Carolina municipalities exercised an influence far beyond the number of their residents as entrepôts of trade, centers of politics and political intrigue, and bases of cultural development. Yet, despite the evidences of urban living, the towns retained a rural flavor. The pace of life was slow. Poultry flitted about; livestock ran loose in the streets. The distinction between town and country in many ways was insignificant.

CHAPTER NINE

# CONCLUSION

Society in colonial North Carolina constituted a kaleidoscopic arrangement of languages, religions, and life-styles. It was a product of European culture developed in a New World environment. The American wilderness modified elements of the Old World and often evoked new societal forms. Still, the colonials clung tenaciously to their European past and imitated their European contemporaries whenever possible.

A noteworthy facet of Carolina society was the varied backgrounds of the settlers. Native Americans were supplanted by Europeans and Africans. The whites originated primarily in England, but large contingents represented such countries as France, Germany, Switzerland, Ireland, and Scotland. The blacks came from various west African states, especially the Guinea Coast, and from the West Indies.

One aspect of European society imported by the dominant white colonials was a hierarchical class structure. The utilization of slavery and indentured servitude reinforced the class system. The greatest extremes of wealth appeared in the Albemarle and particularly the lower Cape Fear area. Nevertheless, North Carolinians seemed much less differentiated than the people of most other English colonies along the seaboard.

The manner of living in North Carolina reflected Old World habits tempered by the New World frontier. Primitive conditions characterized frontier life, and a near subsistence economy prevailed throughout much of the province. Many colonials, however, accumulated sufficient capital to permit a life of relative ease; for some, even luxury. Wealth was a major factor in determining modes of housing, standards of dress, opportunities for education, and attitudes toward cultural enrichment.

The religious experience of North Carolinians similarly reflected varying attitudes. The Anglican Church, or Church of England, was the established church, but it competed less than successfully with numerous other Protestant groups. The diversity of denominational sentiment contributed to a spirit of toleration on the part of the sectaries. Because no one denomination could predominate, all were forced to adopt a policy of tolerance.

Transportation and communication were largely dictated by geographical considerations. Numerous watercourses and the marshy, sandy soil of the eastern portion of the province hindered the progress of transportation. A sparse population compounded such difficulties. However, continuous westward settlement and an increased populace promoted a serviceable transportation network by the outbreak of the Revolution. Communication was similarly delayed. Postal facilities arrived late in the colonial period, as did the printing press and newspaper. Before the Revolution, transportation and communication were generally slow, inefficient, and expensive.

Although North Carolina was predominantly rural, towns—more accurately, villages, in many cases—developed in response to commercial demands. Such towns were often the result of private promotional endeavors, but some were instigated by the colonial government's encouragement of commerce within the province. Town life presented problems of a modern nature, including rubbish removal, sewage disposal, traffic control, fire prevention, and law enforcement. Towns promoted cultural advancement by clustering individuals in a small geographic area which facilitated social interaction and fostered an interchange of ideas. Nevertheless, like most English colonials, North Carolinians remained basically a rural people.

# REFERENCES FOR ADDITIONAL READING

Allcott, John V. *Colonial Homes in North Carolina*. Raleigh: Carolina Charter Tercentenary Commission, 1963.

Anscombe, Francis C. *I Have Called You Friends: The Story of Quakerism in North Carolina*. Boston: Christopher Publishing House, 1959.

Attmore, William. *Journal of a Tour to North Carolina by William Attmore, 1787*. Edited by Lida Tunstall Rodman. James Sprunt Historical Publications, vol. 17, no. 2. Chapel Hill: Published by the University, 1922.

Bailyn, Bernard. *Voyagers to the West: A Passage in the Peopling of America on the Eve of the Revolution*. New York: Alfred A. Knopf, 1986.

Bartram, William. *Travels Through North and South Carolina, Georgia, East and West Florida*. 1791. Reprint, Charlottesville: University of Virginia Press, 1980.

Bassett, John Spencer. *Slavery and Servitude in the Colony of North Carolina*. Baltimore: Johns Hopkins Press, 1896.

Bishir, Catherine W. *North Carolina Architecture*. Chapel Hill: University of North Carolina Press for The Historic Preservation Foundation of North Carolina, Inc., 1990.

Bishir, Catherine W., et al. *Architects and Builders in North Carolina: A History of the Practice of Building*. Chapel Hill: University of North Carolina Press, 1990.

Boyd, William K., ed. *Some Eighteenth Century Tracts Concerning North Carolina*. Raleigh: Edwards & Broughton, 1927.

Brickell, John. *The Natural History of North Carolina*. 1737. Reprint, with biographical notes by Thomas C. Parramore, Murfreesboro, N.C.: Johnson Publishing Company, 1968.

Brooks, Jerome. *Green Leaf and Gold: Tobacco in North Carolina*. Rev. ed. Raleigh: Division of Archives and History, North Carolina Department of Cultural Resources, 1975.

Byrd, William. *William Byrd's Histories of the Dividing Line betwixt Virginia and North Carolina*. Edited by William K. Boyd. Raleigh: North Carolina Historical Commission, 1929.

Cathey, Cornelius O. *Agriculture in North Carolina Before the Civil War*. Raleigh: Division of Archives and History, North Carolina Department of Cultural Resources, 1974.

Clark, Walter, ed. *The State Records of North Carolina*. 16 vols. (11–26). Winston, Goldsboro: State of North Carolina, 1895-1907.

Clonts, F. W. "Travel and Transportation in Colonial North Carolina." *North Carolina Historical Review* 3 (January 1926): 16-35.

Connor, R. D. W. *The Colonial and Revolutionary Periods: 1584-1783*. Vol. 1, *History of North Carolina*. Chicago: Lewis Publishing Company, 1919.

Craig, James H. *The Arts and Crafts in North Carolina, 1689-1840*. Winston-Salem: Museum of Early Southern Decorative Arts, Old Salem, Inc., 1965.

Crittenden, Charles Christopher. *The Commerce of North Carolina, 1763-1789*. New Haven: Yale University Press, 1936.

Crow, Jeffrey J. *The Black Experience in Revolutionary North Carolina*. Raleigh: Division of Archives and History, North Carolina Department of Cultural Resources, 1977.

Crow, Jeffrey J., Paul D. Escott, and Flora J. Hatley. *A History of African Americans in North Carolina*. Raleigh: Division of Archives and History, North Carolina Department of Cultural Resources, 1992.

Ekirch, A. Roger. *"Poor Carolina": Politics and Society in Colonial North Carolina, 1729-1776*. Chapel Hill: University of North Carolina Press, 1981.

Fenn, Elizabeth A., and Peter H. Wood. *Natives & Newcomers: The Way We Lived in North Carolina before 1770*. Chapel Hill: University of North Carolina Press for the North Carolina Department of Cultural Resources, 1983.

Fischer, David Hackett. *Albion's Seed: Four British Folkways in America*. New York: Oxford University Press, 1989.

Fries, Adelaide L., et al., eds. *Records of the Moravians in North Carolina*. 11 vols. Raleigh: North Carolina Historical Commission, 1922-1969.

Gallman, James M. "Determinants of Age at Marriage in Colonial Perquimans County, North Carolina." *William and Mary Quarterly*, 3d ser., 39 (January 1982): 176–191.

Hall, Clement. *A Collection of Many Christian Experiences, Sentences, and Several Places of Scripture Improved.* 1753. Reprint, with an introduction by William S. Powell, Raleigh: State Department of Archives and History, 1961.

Hazard, Ebenezer. "The Journal of Ebenezer Hazard in North Carolina, 1777 and 1778." Edited by Hugh B. Johnston. *North Carolina Historical Review* 36 (July 1959): 358–381.

Higginbotham, Don, ed. *The Papers of James Iredell.* 2 vols. Raleigh: Division of Archives and History, Department of Cultural Resources, 1976.

Johnson, Guion G. *Ante-Bellum North Carolina: A Social History.* Chapel Hill: University of North Carolina Press, 1937.

Johnston, Frances Benjamin, and Thomas T. Waterman. *The Early Architecture of North Carolina.* Chapel Hill: University of North Carolina Press, 1941.

Kay, Marvin L. Michael, and Lorin Lee Cary. "Class, Mobility, and Conflict in North Carolina on the Eve of the Revolution." In *The Southern Experience in the American Revolution,* edited by Jeffrey J. Crow and Larry E. Tise, 109-151. Chapel Hill: University of North Carolina Press, 1978.

———. "A Demographic Analysis of Colonial North Carolina with Special Emphasis on the Slave and Black Populations." In *Black Americans in North Carolina and the South,* edited by Jeffrey J. Crow and Flora J. Hatley, 71-121. Chapel Hill: University of North Carolina Press, 1984.

Knight, Edgar W. *Public School Education in North Carolina.* Boston: Houghton Mifflin Co., 1916.

Lawson, John. *A New Voyage to Carolina.* Edited by Hugh T. Lefler. Chapel Hill: University of North Carolina Press, 1967.

Lee, E. Lawrence. *The Lower Cape Fear in Colonial Days.* Chapel Hill: University of North Carolina Press, 1965.

Lefler, Hugh T., and Albert R. Newsome. *North Carolina: The History of a Southern State.* 3d ed. Chapel Hill: University of North Carolina Press, 1973.

Lefler, Hugh T., and William S. Powell. *Colonial North Carolina: A History.* New York: Charles Scribner's Sons, 1973.

Lennon, Donald R. "The Development of Town Government in Colonial North Carolina." In *Of Tar Heel Towns, Shipbuilders, Reconstructionists and Alliancemen: Papers in North Carolina History,* edited by Joseph F. Steelman, 1-25. East Carolina University Publications in History, vol. 5. Greenville, N.C.: East Carolina University Publications, Department of History, 1981.

REFERENCES FOR ADDITIONAL READING

Lennon, Donald R., and Ida Brooks Kellam, eds. *The Wilmington Town Book: 1743-1778*. Raleigh: Division of Archives and History, North Carolina Department of Cultural Resources, 1973.

Lewis, Henry W. "Horses and Horseman in Northampton before 1900." *North Carolina Historical Review* 51 (spring 1974): 125-148.

Lewis, Johanna Miller. "Women Artisans of the Backcountry, 1753-1790." *North Carolina Historical Review* 68 (July 1991): 214-236.

Leyburn, James G. *The Scotch-Irish: A Social History*. Chapel Hill: University of North Carolina Press, 1962.

Logan, William. "William Logan's Journal of a Journey to Georgia, 1745." *Pennsylvania Magazine of History and Biography* 36 (1912): 1-16.

Mathews, Alice E. *Society in Revolutionary North Carolina*. Raleigh: Division of Archives and History, North Carolina Department of Cultural Resources, 1976.

Merrens, Harry Roy. *Colonial North Carolina in the Eighteenth Century: A Study in Historical Geography*. Chapel Hill: University of North Carolina Press, 1964.

Meyer, Duane G. *The Highland Scots of North Carolina, 1732-1776*. Chapel Hill: University of North Carolina Press, 1961.

Miranda, Francisco de. *The New Democracy in America: Travels of Francisco de Miranda in the United States, 1783-1784*. Translated by Judson P. Wood and edited by John S. Ezell. Norman, Okla.: University of Oklahoma Press, 1963.

Morgan, Jacob L., Bachman S. Brown Jr., and John Hall, eds. *History of the Lutheran Church in North Carolina*. Salisbury: United Evangelical Lutheran Synod of North Carolina, 1953.

Parramore, Thomas C. *Cradle of the Colony: The History of Chowan County and Edenton, North Carolina*. Edenton: Chamber of Commerce, 1967.

Paschal, George W. *History of North Carolina Baptists*. 2 vols. Raleigh: General Board, North Carolina Baptist State Convention, 1930-1955.

Paschal, Herbert R., Jr. *A History of Colonial Bath*. Raleigh: Edwards and Broughton, 1955.

Paul, Charles L. "Colonial Beaufort." *North Carolina Historical Review* 42 (spring 1965): 139-152.

———. "Factors in the Economy of Colonial Beaufort." *North Carolina Historical Review* 44 (spring 1967): 111-134.

Powell, William S., ed. *The Correspondence of William Tryon and Other Selected Papers.* 2 vols. Raleigh: Division of Archives and History, Department of Cultural Resources, 1980-1981.

Quincy, Josiah, Jr. "The Southern Journal of Josiah Quincy, Junior, 1773." Massachusetts Historical Society, *Proceedings* 49 (1916): 424-481.

Ramsey, Robert W. *Carolina Cradle: Settlement of the Northwest Carolina Frontier, 1747-1762.* Chapel Hill: University of North Carolina Press, 1964.

Rights, Douglas L. *The American Indian in North Carolina.* Durham: Duke University Press, 1947; 2d ed. Winston-Salem: John F. Blair, 1957.

Roberts, B. W. C. "Cockfighting: An Early Entertainment in North Carolina." *North Carolina Historical Review* 42 (summer 1965): 306-314.

Saunders, William L., ed. *The Colonial Records of North Carolina.* 10 vols. Raleigh: State of North Carolina, 1886-1890.

Schaw, Janet. *Journal of a Lady of Quality.* Edited by Evangeline W. Andrews, in collaboration with Charles M. Andrews. New Haven: Yale University Press, 1921.

Schoepf, Johann David. *Travels in the Confederation, 1783-1784.* 2 vols. Translated and edited by Alfred J. Morrison. Philadelphia: W. J. Campbell, 1911.

Shryock, Richard H. *Medicine and Society in America, 1660-1860.* New York: New York University Press, 1960.

Smyth, John Ferdinand Dalziel. *A Tour in the United States of America.* 2 vols. London: G. Robinson, J. Robson, and J. Sewell, 1784.

South, Stanley A. *Indians in North Carolina.* Raleigh: State Department of Archives and History, 1959.

Spindel, Donna J. "Women's Civil Actions in the North Carolina Higher Courts, 1670-1730." *North Carolina Historical Review* 71 (April 1994): 151-173.

Spruill, Julia Cherry. *Women's Life and Work in the Southern Colonies.* Chapel Hill: University of North Carolina Press, 1938.

Swaim, Douglas, ed. *Carolina Dwelling: Towards Preservation of Place, In Celebration of the North Carolina Vernacular Landscape.* Raleigh: North Carolina State University, 1978.

Sweet, William Warren. *Men of Zeal: The Romance of American Methodist Beginnings.* New York: Abingdon Press, 1935.

———. *Religion in Colonial America.* New York: Cooper Square Publishers, Inc., 1965.

Tiffany, Nina Moore, ed. *The Letters of James Murray, Loyalist.* Boston: Printed, not published, 1901.

Watson, Alan D. "Society and Economy in Colonial Edgecombe County." *North Carolina Historical Review* 50 (summer 1973): 231-255.

———. "Orphanage in Colonial North Carolina: Edgecombe as a Case Study." *North Carolina Historical Review* 52 (spring 1975): 105-119.

———. "Public Poor Relief in Colonial North Carolina." *North Carolina Historical Review* 54 (autumn 1977): 347-366.

———. "Women in Colonial North Carolina: Overlooked and Underestimated." *North Carolina Historical Review* 58 (winter 1981): 1-22.

Watson, Harry. *An Independent People: The Way We Lived in North Carolina, 1770-1820.* Chapel Hill: University of North Carolina Press for the North Carolina Department of Cultural Resources, 1983.

Woodmason, Charles. *The Carolina Backcountry on the Eve of the Revolution: The Journal and Other Writings of Charles Woodmason, Anglican Itinerant.* Edited by Richard Hooker. Chapel Hill: University of North Carolina Press for the Institute of Early American History and Culture at Williamsburg, Va., 1953.

# INDEX

## A

Adams, James, 71

African Americans: arrival of, 6; continuation of African culture among, 7, 21; diseases among, 67, 70; education of, 73, 98; and horse racing, 15; number of, 6; obligation of, to work on roads, 101; origins of, 128; relations of, with whites, 8, 26; religion among, 85, 97-98; as servants, 20; in urban areas, 39, 124. *See also* Free blacks; Slaves

Alamance, Battle of, 39, 82

Alamance County, 90

Albemarle, 6; economic conditions in 78, 128; education of blacks in, 73; granting of, to Lords Proprietors, 1; isolation of, 113; religious groups in, 89-90, 94; slavery in, 7, 12; trade with, 110

Albemarle Sound, 1, 85; ferry service across, 106-107, 109, 113

Alexander, Hezekiah, 51-52; home of, pictured, 52

Allen, George, 35

Allen House (Alamance Battlefield), pictured, 48

Alphin, Robert, 79

Ancrum and Schaw Company, 64

Andrew (slave of John Culpepper), 41

Anglican Church: aids poor, 78; educational efforts of, 70-71, 73, 75; as established church, 83-84, 95, 129; ministers, 85-86, 88; missionaries to blacks and Native Americans, 97-98; missionaries estimate number of Quakers, 89; regional appeal of, 126; relations of, with Baptists, 93-94; requests to, for resident bishop, 85; role of, at Queen's College, 76

Anne, Queen (of England), 84

Anson County, 5, 29, 107

Arnal, Moses, 36

Arndt, Johann Gottfried, 90

Asbury, Francis, 94

Attmore, William, 38

Attorneys. *See* Lawyers

Avery, Waightstill, 14

## B

Baker, Henry, 30

Baker, Joshua, 33

Baker, Ruth, 30

Baptists, 89, 93-94, 97

Barnett, John, 73, 97

Barrow, William, 30

Bartram, William, 117

Batchelor, Edward, 43-44

Bath: control of development in, 121; description of, 112-113; Edward Teach in, 113-114; effects of New Bern's growth on, 115; establishement of, 1; fences in, 122; legislature meets in, 126; Palmer-Marsh house in, pictured, 50; St. Thomas Church in, pictured, 84; school for blacks in, considered, 73; transportation links to, 101, 107, 109

Beaufort: description of, 113; educational philanthropy in, 71; effects of New Bern's growth on, 115; incorporation of, 1; law enforcement in, 96; local government in, 119; racing in streets of, 122; seafood in, 56; town boundaries assessed in, 120

Beaufort County, 45, 93

Belinda (slave), 43

Bell, Elizabeth, 36

Bell, Thomas, 73

Ben (slave of Hardie Maund), 38

Bennehan, Mrs., 28

Bennehan, Richard, 28

Bennett, John, 72

Berkeley, William, pictured, 2

Berkenpine, John, 81

Bertie County: economic conditions in, 8; ferry service in, 107; population in, 19; servants in, 20; slavery in 20, 41

Bethabara, 71, 95, 118, 124

Bethania, 71, 118

Biddle, Jacob, 81

Birth rates, 25

Blackall, Abraham, 69

Blackbeard. *See* Teach, Edward

Blacks. *See* African Americans; Free blacks; Slaves

Bladen County, 5

Blair, John, 85

Blair, Nelly, 27

Boazman, Elizabeth, 26

Boman, Thomas, 42

Bond, Richard, 79

Bonn, Jacob, 69

Boulton, James, 27

Boyd, Adam, 23

Boyd, Jennet, 29

Boyd, John, 86

Braddock, Edward, 92

Bradley, Martha, 58

Braun, Michael, 50-52; home of, pictured, 52

Bray, Thomas, 85

Brett, Daniel, 86

Brickell, John, 23, 78, 100

Bridges, 104-105, 121

Briggs, James, 33

*British Housewife, The*, 58

Brunswick County, 12, 20, 97

Brunswick Town: description of, 115; local government in, 119; Moravians trade with, 103-104; postal service in, 109; St. Philips Church in, pictured, 116

Burgess, Thomas, 73

Burgwin, John, 50, 53, 121

Burgwin-Wright House (Wilmington), 50

Burnby, John, 41

Burrington, George, 1

Bute County, 97, 105

Byrd, William: describes Carolinians, 16-17, 37, homes, 48; encounters black family, 9-10; on New England rum, 57; observes disease, 70

# C

Cabarrus County, 90

Cain, Michael, 32

Caldwell, David, 75, 93

Callaway, Caleb, 30

Campbell, James, 92, 120

Campbell, John, 69

Campbell, Robert, 82

Campellton, 116-117

Cannon, Richard, 81

Cape Fear: British raid on, 115; economic conditions in, 128; education of blacks in, 73; Highland Scots in, 5; housework in, 64; indolence among residents of, 17; miscegenation in, 26-27; planter's home in, 49; religion in, 96; settlement of, 1, 3, 6, 115; slavery in 7, 12, 20, 37; socioeconomic classes in, 14

Cape Fear River: Brunswick Town on, 115; description of, 10; ferry service on, 106; Highland Scots along, 92; mouth of, map, 11; navigation problems on, 115

Carolina Charter, pictured, 2

Carteret County, 19, 68, 78, 93

Cary, Thomas, 84

Cashie River, 105

Castle Hayne, 105

Catawba Indians, 67, 117

Catawba River, 5, 92, 106

Catholics, 83, 94-95, 98

Chadwick, Ephraim, 81

Champion, Orlando, 79

Charles II, 1; pictured, frontispiece

Charlotte, 51, 76, 117, 119

Charlton, Jasper, 13

Chatham County, 90

Cherokee Indians, 67, 117

Childsburgh, 117

Chloe (slave of Hardie Maund), 38

Chowan County, 113; aid for smallpox victims in, 80; Baptists in, 93; education in, 71; free blacks in, 21; lawyers in, 13; poor relief in, 78; population in, 19; slavery in, 20

Chowan River, 27, 71

Church of England. See Anglican Church

Church of the Brethren. See Dunkers

Clothing, 61-64

Cockfighting, 15

Cogdell, Charles, 35

Compleat Housewife, The, 58

Connor, Morris, 28

Conway, Mary, 72

Coogan, Mary, 34

Cooper, Anthony Ashley, pictured, 2

Corbin, Jean, 40

Corbinton, 117

# F

Faughy, Ann, 35-36
Fayetteville, 117. *See also* Cross Creek
Ferries, 105-107, 109
Finlay, Hugh, 109
Finny, Christian, 36
Fire hazards, 123-124
Flat Rock congregation (Church of the Brethern), 91
Food, 54-56, 58-60
Fox, George, 89
Frank (slave of Seth Sothel and Thomas Pollock), 21
Franklin, Benjamin, 4
Fraternity Church of the Brethern (near Winston-Salem), 91
Free blacks, 9-10, 21, 40. *See also* African Americans
French and Indian War, 76, 82
French settlers, 3
Frey, Christian, 95
Friedburg, 71
Fundamental Constitutions, 6
Furniture, 54

# G

Gainor, Mary, 62
Gainor, William, 62
Gale, Katherine, 33
Gambling, 15-16
Gardens, 53-54
Garzia, John, 94
Geekie, James, 69
George Junior (slave of Jean Innes), 21
German Reformed Church, 89-90
German settlers, 3-4, 6, 75, 90
Gibbs, Walterman, 34
Godbe, Cary, 36

Gomez, Moses, 34
Gordon, Mary, 39
Goss, Fredrick, 81
Grace Church (Rowan County), 90
Graffenried, Baron Christoph von, 1, 3, 113
Granade, John, 81
Granville, Earl, 91, 113
Granville County, 10, 29, 86
Great Wagon Road, 5, 117
Green, John, 33
Green, Rebecca, 69
Green, Samuel, 69
Griffin, Charles, 71
Guilford County, 90, 93, 102
Guy, Elizabeth, 81

# H

Halifax, 117; ball in, 14; description of, 116; fire prevention in, 124; local government in, 119-120; transportation link to, 101
Halifax County, 67, 93
Hall, Clement, 85-86, 94
Harnett, Cornelius, 25-26, 68
Harnett, Mary, 25
Harnett County, 5
Hatteras Indians, 98
Hawks, John, 51
Haw River, 106
Hayne, Anne, 29
Hayne, Fincher, 29
Hazard, Ebenezer, 37, 107
Hecklefield, John, 40
Hermitage plantation, 53
Heron, Benjamin, 105, 123
Hertford, 119
Hertford County, 107, 119
Hibbs, Jonathan, 33
Hicks, John, 80

Lenox, Robert, 69

Lewis, Richard, 33

Liberty Hall Academy, 76-77

Liddle, John, 33

Logan, William, 59

Log College, 75

London (slave), 43

Lords Proprietors: encourage formation of towns, 112; encourage slavery, 6; favor South Carolina, 84; on religion, 83; royal grant to, 1

Loss, John, 81

Lovett, Richard, 34

Lovick, Thomas, 32

Lowlanders, 5, 92. *See also* Scottish settlers

Lutherans, 89-90

Lyon, John, 121

Lytle, Thomas, 34

## M

McAden, Hugh, 92

McAlister, Isabella, 23

McCarthy, Florence, 74

McCome, Elinor, 35

McCorkle, Samuel E., 93

McGehe, Joseph, 29

McGehe, Mary, 29

McGlothlin, John, 35

McLeod, John, 92

McLorinan, Catherine, 29

McLorinan, Henry, 29

Manuell (slave of Seth Sothel and Thomas Pollock), 21

Martin, Josiah, 45, 120

Martin County, 45, 93, 103

Mashburn, Mr., 71

Mason, Caleb, 121

Masonic Order, 126

Mattamuskeet Indians, 98

Maule, Patrick, 30

Maund, Hardie, 38

Maury, James, 4

Maynard, Robert, 114

Mecklenburg County: county seat established in, 119; education in, 76; ferry service in, 107; Presbyterians in, 92; transportation link to, 102

Methodists, 89, 94-95, 97

Milner, James, 14, 77

Miranda, Francisco de, 14, 16, 24

Mitchell, Abraham, 35

Mittam's Point, 119

Moir, James, 71

Moll (slave of Thomas Pollock), 21

Monroe, Captain, 22

Moore, George, 12, 121

Moore, Maurice, 1; pictured, 3

Moore County, 5

Moravians, 90; architecture of, 50; contact with Native Americans by, 118; description of, 91-92; education of, 71; establish Salem, 118; fire prevention among, 124; illness and disease among, 67; immigration of, 6, 91; increase in number of, 89; physicians among, 69; postal service to, 110; trade by, 103-104, 110, 115

Mortimer, John, 69

Moseley, Edward, 72, 76-77

Moseley, Miss, 22

Moultrie, William, 119

Murray, James, 13, 22

Myers, John, 27

## N

Nash, Abner, 15

Native Americans, 128; conflict with settlers, 3-4, 89; contact with Moravians, 118; diseases among, 67; education of, 73; engage in fur trade, 1; missionaries to, 85, 97-98; similarities of western settlers to, 96

Naval stores, 10

Neuse River, 1, 106, 113

Neuse-Trent area, 12

New Bern: becomes capital, 126; description of, 113; economic growth in, 115; education in, 74-75; fences in 122; fire prevention in, 124; fund raising for bridge in, 105; Governor Tryon moves to, 115; hanging in, 94; hat maker in, 63; local government in, 119-120; market regulations in, 125; Masonic Order in, 126; Moravians trade with, 103-104; newspapers in, 108, 126; quarantine ships off, 80; settlement at, 1; slavery in, 38-39, 45, 125; social system in, 14; transportation links to, 101-102, 107, 109; Tryon Palace in, 50

*New Bern North Carolina Gazette*, 108

*New Bern North Carolina Magazine; or, Universal Intelligencer*, 108

Newbold-White House (Perquimans County), 50

New Carthage, 115

New Garden, 90

New Hanover County: ferry service in, 106; free blacks in, 21; ministers in, 86, 92; prenuptial contracts in, 23; relief for smallpox victims in, 80; slavery in, 12, 20;

New River, 106-107, 119

New Liverpool, 115

Newman, Thomas, 94

Newspapers, 108-109, 126, 129

Newton, 115

Newton, Christian, 27

Nicholson, William, 34

Nixonton, 119

Noble, Samuel, 35

Northampton County, 10, 73, 89

Northeast Cape Fear River: drawbridge over, 105; ferry crossing over, 106; road connection to, 102; suicide in, 43; Welsh settlers along, 3

Northwest Cape Fear River, 117

Nussman, Adolph, 90

# O

Ocracoke Inlet, 114, 119

Ocracoke Island, 114

O'Hara, Mary, 35

Onslow County, 19, 119

Orange County, 29, 117

Orange Presbytery, 93

Ormond, Wyriot, 77

Orphans, 25-26, 72, 80

Outer Banks, 10

# P

Paine, John, 99

Palmer, Paul, 93

Palmer-Marsh House (Bath), 50

Pamlico River, 1, 3, 109

Pamlico Sound, 119

Pasquotank County, 71, 89, 119

Pasquotank River, 107

Patillo, Henry, 93

Paul, Joseph, 29

Perquimans County: county seat established in, 119; marriages in, 23; Newbold-White House in, 50; Quakers in, 89; slavery in, 20

Perquimans River, 107
Peter (slave of Jean Corbin), 40
Pettigrew, Charles, 75
Pfifer, John, 76
Phillips, James, 33
Pilmore, Joseph, 94, 107; pictured, 95
Pitt County, 19, 25, 45, 107
Pollock, Cullen, 76
Pollock, Thomas, 21
Portis, Thomas, 27
Portsmouth, 119
Postal service, 107, 109-110, 129
Prenuptial contracts, 23
Presbyterians: early, in colony, 92; and education, 75-76; on gender roles in marriage, 24; increase in number of, 89; in Ireland, 5; organization of, 93
*Present State of Virginia, The*, 95
Purvine, Rachel, 79

## Q

Quakers: antislavery views of, 40, 98; early dominance by, 83; increase in number of, 89-90; opposition by, to established church, 84; outnumbering of, by Baptists, 93; role of women among, 24
Queen's College, 76, 119
Queen's Museum, 76
Quince, Richard, 12
Quincy, Josiah, Jr., 37, 96
Quomons (slave of Benjamin Reed), 40

## R

Rainbough, Nancy, 22
Rainsford, John, 85

Randolph County, 90
Recreation, 14-16
Reed, Benjamin, 40
Reed, James, 75, 77, 94
Reed, William, 34
Regulators, 82
Richmond (slave of Ancrum and Schaw Co.), 64
Richmond County, 5
Ricks, James, 73
Rigby, Hugh, 81
Roanoke Indians, 98
Roanoke River, 56, 101, 116
Robeson County, 5
Robinson, Esther, 81
Robinson, William, 92
Ross, Mr., 69
Ross, Mrs., 69
Rowan County: Braun House in, 50, pictured, 52; county seat of, 117; education for apprentices in, 73; ferry service in, 107; German settlers in, 90; sick and poor relief in, 80-81; spinners in, 25; transportation link to, 102
Russellborough, 53
Rutherford, John, 27, 74, 121
Ryley, Mabel, 34

## S

St. James Church (Wilmington), 99, 126
St. John's Lutheran Church (Cabarrus County), 90
St. John's Lutheran Church (Rowan County), 90
St. John's Parish (Carteret County), 78-79
St. Luke's Parish (Rowan County), 80

St. Paul's Church (Edenton), pictured, 87

St. Paul's Parish (Chowan County): absence of Catholics in, 94; education in, 71; minister in, 85; poor relief in, 78-79; standards of weights and measures in, 88

St. Philips Church (Brunswick Town), pictured, 116

St. Philips Parish (Brunswick County), 97

St. Thomas Church (Bath), pictured, 84

St. Thomas Parish (Beaufort County), 94

Salem, 117; architecture in 50; description of, 118; education in, 71; fire prevention in 124

Salisbury, 117, 119, 122

Salter, James, 34

Sampson County, 5

Sandy Creek Association, 93

Sandy Creek Church, 93

Schaw, Janet: conveyance of, on Northeast Cape Fear, 101; on education, 74; on families, 25, 27; on indolence of Cape Fear residents, 17; on living conditions of slaves, 37-38; on plantation life, 49; on social equality in Lower Cape Fear, 14; on street conditions in Wilmington, 122

Schoepf, Johann, 40

Schubert, Dr., 69

Scipio (slave of Thomas Pollock), 21

Scotch-Irish settlers, 3-4; education stimulated by, 75; reasons for emigration of, 5; religious services for, 92; routes taken by, 6; views of Presbyterian, on gender roles, 24; in Wilmington, 116

Scotland County, 5

Scottish settlers, 4-5, 24, 92, 116

Sharp, Walter, 41

Sheriff, Matilda, 35

Short, Peter, 34

Sinclear Junior (slave of Jean Innes), 21

Single Brothers House (Salem), 50

Slaves, 8, 31, 128; attitude of Quakers toward, 40; cabins of, 49, pictured, 49; clothing of, 38; diet of, 38, 59-60; families of, 21-22; hiring of, 39; insurrection by, 45-46; introduction of, into colony, 6; living conditions of, 37; manumission of, 39-40; marriages among, 9; origins of, 7; as part of colonial households, 20, 29; population of, 11-12; punishment of, for violating town ordinances, 122; regulation of, 32, 37, 39, 45; religious activities of, 9; resistance by, 9, 41; runaway, 9, 41-43, pictured 42; subjugation of, to masters, 9; in urban areas, 39, 124-125. *See also* African Americans

Smith, E., 58

Smith, Faithy, 82

Smith, Michael, 86

Smith, Rachel, 36

Smyth, J. F. D., 41

Sneads Ferry, 106

Snoad, Elizabeth, 30

Society for the Propagation of the Gospel in Foreign Parts (SPG), 85-86, 97

Sothel, Seth, 21

Spangenberg, August Gottlieb, 91, 103; pictured, 91

Stanly, John Carruthers, 27

Stanly, John Wright, 21, 27

Stanly County, 90

Stearns, Shubal, 93

Williams, Judith, 33

Williams, Robert, 42

Wilmington, 113; Burgwin-Wright House in, 50; fires in, 123; growth of, 115-116; Jewish residents of, 95; law enforcement in, 96-97; legislature meets in, 126; local government in, 119-120, 125-126; Masonic Order in, 126; newspapers in, 108, 126; philanthropy in, 99; physicians in, 69; public works in, 121-122; sale of food in, 25, 125; Scottish and Scotch-Irish settlers in, 116; slavery in 38-39, 45, 124-125; transportation links to, 101- 102, 107, 109

*Wilmington Cape Fear Mercury*, 108

*Wilmington North Carolina Gazette and Weekly Post Boy*, 108

*Wilmington Town Book, The*, 120

Wimberly, 119

Windsor, 105, 119

Winton, 119

Winwright, James, 71-72

Woodmason, Charles, 22, 83, 96

Woodstock, 119

# Y

Yadkin River, 5-6, 92, 106

York (slave), 43

# Z

Zion Lutheran Church (Rowan County), 90